Habitats

Grades 4-6

Written by Patricia Urie
Illustrated by S&S Learning Materials

ISBN 1-55035-629-1
Copyright 1999
Revised January 2006
All Rights Reserved * Printed in Canada

Published in the United States by:
On the Mark Press
3909 Witmer Road PMB 175
Niagara Falls, New York
14305
www.onthemarkpress.com

Published in Canada by:
S&S Learning Materials
15 Dairy Avenue
Napanee, Ontario
K7R 1M4
www.sslearning.com

Look For OTHER SCIENCE UNITS

Habitats

Table of Contents

Habitats

Unit Overview

This resource is divided into seven components. The topics are best covered sequentially, however each component may be used alone. Many of the activities can be integrated into other areas of the curriculum.

Component	This component examines the concepts related to...	The main investigative activities will require the student to...
What is Ecology?	• the science of ecology as the science interested in the study of the homes of plants and animals	• become a 'Junior Ecologist' • set up, maintain and observe mini-habitats (optional)
A Habitat is a Home	• habitats and the basic needs of living things • the factors that affect plants and animals living in specific habitats	• investigate a backyard habitat • record observations in the form of a tally chart, drawing, map and graph
Food Chains	• food chains, food webs and the role of various living things in a food chain • energy, plant growth, producers and consumers, etc.	• construct food chains and webs
Each to Its Niche	• the term 'ecological niche' as it applies to the role of every living thing in maintaining balance in nature	• observe wood lice and record your observations • plan and conduct a scientific investigation of wood lice
The Earth's Biomes	• the major biomes of the earth, the plant and animal life found in each and the ways plants and animals in these regions survive	• prepare a short research project about one of the earth's biomes
Adaptation	• the various structural adaptations which allow animals and plants to survive in their habitats	• observe and describe the special adaptations of animals and plants to their environments • investigate the adaptations of fish
Habitat Helpers	• the positive and negative effects of human behavior on habitats • the importance of preserving the habitats of living things	• complete a short report about an endangered species • experiment and draw conclusions about air pollution • design an ecology game using the concepts related to habitats • plan and deliver an oral presentation

Habitats

Teacher Input

Teacher suggestions and resources can be found at the beginning of each component. These pages give a brief overview of each topic, the learning expectations for the component and ideas for planning ahead and implementing the section. The implementation suggestions are presented as ideas only. It is not intended that any or all be implemented to use the activity pages.

Students will be expect to:

1. Identify, through observation, various factors that affect plants and animals in a specific habitat.

2. Classify organisms according to their role in a food chain.

3. Demonstrate an understanding of a food chain as a system in which energy from the sun is eventually transferred to animals.

4. Describe the structural adaptations of plants and animals that demonstrate a response of living things to their environment.

5. Recognize that plants and animals live in specific habitats because they are dependent on those habitats and have adapted to them.

6. Classify plants and animals observed in local habitats according to similarities and differences.

7. Formulate questions about and identify the needs of animals and plants in a particular habitat and explore possible answers to these questions and ways of meeting these needs.

8. Use appropriate vocabulary and science terminology when describing investigations, explorations and observations.

9. Compile data gathered through investigation, in order to record and present results, using tally charts, tables and graphs.

10. Communicate the procedures and results of investigations.

11. Describe ways in which humans are dependent on plants and animals.

12. Describe ways in which humans can affect the natural world.

13. Construct food chains that include different plant and animal species.

14. Show the effects on plants and animals of the loss of their natural habitats.

15. Investigate ways in which the extinction of a plant or animal species affects the rest of the natural community as well as humans.

16. Understand that the information we have and continue to gain about plants and animals, their relationships to one another and their roles in the environment are due to the science of ecology.

17. Understand that the study of ecology is important to an understanding of environmental problems and possible solutions to those problems.

18. Understand that scientists gain information through observation and experimentation.

Habitats

19. Have an understanding of the purpose of the activities and approach them like young scientists.

20. Plan investigations and identify variables that need to be held constant to ensure fair and accurate testing.

Vocabulary

What is Ecology?:
ecology, ecologist, investigate, botanist, suited, cactus, scientist, community, source, protection

A Habitat is a Home:
environment, habitat, ecosystem, shelter, survive, climate, compete, soil

Food Chains:
(card 1) carnivore, omnivore, herbivore, insectivore, secondary consumer, producer, primary consumer, energy, predator
(card 2) carbon dioxide, glucose, photosynthesis, oxygen, chlorophyll, absorbed, substance, nutrients

Each to Its Niche:
ecological niche, thrive, balance, species, adapted, reproduce

The Earth's Biomes:
biome, vegetation, tropical, polar, coniferous, deciduous, rain forest, savanna, humid, pampas, prairies, plains, steppe, tundra, altitude, wetland, temperature, precipitation

Adaptations:
feature, adaptation, mammal, blubber, camouflage, conserve, aestivation, hibernation, agile, migration

Habitat Helpers:
endangered, extinct, pollute, pesticide, insecticide, chemicals, pest, interfere, exterminate, global, fertilizer, conserve

Planning Ahead

A study of habitats is best undertaken in the spring or fall when plants and small animals are easily obtained and students can plan and make investigations.

Begin collecting the resources on the checklist below in advance. Ask students to help.

- ✓ books, magazines (about plants, animals, adaptations, ecology, rain forest, polar regions, desert, savanna, etc.)
- ✓ films, filmstrips, videos
- ✓ kits
- ✓ old calendars, magazines (for pictures)
- ✓ encyclopedias of science
- ✓ computer software ("Magic School Bus" series is very good)

Habitats

✓ mini-habitat supplies (see Setting Up Mini-habitats)
✓ specimens (plants, animal teeth, skins, fur, seeds, shells, pine cones, etc.)

Plan for the storage of student work i.e. duo-tangs, binders, etc. or folders decorated by the students.

Student evaluation pages 10 to 13 can be cut in half and made into a small booklet.

Implementation

As each component is introduced, duplicate the student activity pages and make into small booklets which will be easy to evaluate and display.

Use the picture book listed in the Resources section of each component or the information cards as 'springboards' for introducing each component.

Integrate some of the activities into other areas of the curriculum or allow the students to complete them at home.

Make charts of the vocabulary words and display them in the classroom as each component is introduced. Have the students add the words to their vocabulary pages (16 & 17.) Use the words for word study activities.

Update the Resource pages by adding the titles of resources such as films, kits, books, etc. that you find helpful throughout the book. Make quick notes about the suitability of each resource for future reference.

Setting Up Classroom Habitats

Rationale

Although the greatest part of this resource can be implemented easily without live specimens, setting up one or two habitats in the classroom will enhance and make the concepts being taught more meaningful and interesting. Students will enjoy collecting specimens and setting up and maintaining 'mini-habitats' in the classroom. Simple habitats can be set up with little expense. For the enthusiast there are many good books available; highly recommended is Hickman's 'Habitats.' (see Resources)

If you ask students to set up classroom habitats, they should be well informed beforehand. They should discuss which specimens are suitable and be asked to treat the environment with care when removing specimens. Most specimens can be found in backyard areas, however students may wish to visit a field or wooded area. They should be made aware of how and where to collect plant and animal specimens and it is recommended that they do so under adult supervision. Small specimens are best. It should be stressed that specimens will be returned to their natural habitat at the end of the book.

Habitats

Students should be instructed about the need to wash their hands immediately after handling plants, animals and soils, etc. Depending on the contents of the habitats and the age of the students, it might be a safe practice to allow the students to remove animals from habitats only under supervision.

Materials

1. Small aquariums are the most adaptable containers for mini-habitats, and slightly broken ones can be put to use for habitats for small rodents, insects and plants etc. The contents are easily viewed and labels, etc. can be attached easily. The aquariums make great storage containers for activity cards, theme books, plant supplies, etc. when not being used for habitats.
2. Large pickle or mayonnaise jars also make great habitats, either standing or lying on their sides. They can often be obtained from restaurants.
3. Large clear, plastic candy containers are ideal.
4. Old lamp shades or cardboard boxes with windows cut in them can be wrapped with screening materials to make excellent habitats for insects, etc.
5. A spray bottle of water is necessary to keep some of the habitats moist. Any plant paraphernalia like soil, pots, hand digging tools and watering cans will also prove useful.
6. Students often have plant, insect and bird guides, etc. It is wise to try to collect them ahead as they will prove very useful. Most school libraries also have copies.

Mini-Habitats

1. The simple habitat and the terrarium which follow are easy to set up. They were chosen because the contents can be easily obtained and both can be set up with a minimum of expense and maintenance. It is recommended that you set up at least one and preferably both.
2. The student investigation 'Wonderful Wood Lice' requires working with wood lice (also known as pill bugs or sow bugs.) By setting up this habitat, the wood lice will be readily available when you need them.

Moist Woodland Terrarium

A terrarium is quite easy to make. It is a covered container (clean) which contains a community of miniature plants. Once set up it will require a minimum of attention.

<u>Materials Required:</u>

1. a glass or plastic container (old aquarium, large jar, etc.) with room for plants to grow
2. a removable plastic cover (glass, plexiglass, plastic wrap, etc.)
3. coarse sand or gravel for drainage
4. soil
5. plants such as ferns, ivy, mosses, fungi, root cuttings of begonia, coleus, etc.

Habitats

Directions for Making Terrarium:

1. Place one cm (0.5 inches) of gravel, sand or a combination in the bottom of the aquarium or jar (a jar is very suitable placed on its side).
2. Add two cm (one inch) of moist potting soil or other mix (preferably one third soil, one third peat moss, one third sand).
3. Make holes in the soil and put seeds and small plants in place.
4. Place moss around plants or in corners to retain moisture and add beauty to the terrariums.
5. Add rocks, small bits of rotting logs, toadstools, etc. for interest.
6. Spray with water from an atomiser.
7. Cover with glass or plastic. Do not place a covered terrarium in direct sunlight.
8. Water only once a week or when the soil dries out. If too much moisture accumulates, remove the lid a little at a time.

Wood Lice Habitat

Materials Required:

1. a glass or plastic container (old aquarium, large jar, etc.)
2. coarse sand or gravel for drainage
3. soil
4. wood lice (pill bugs easily found under rocks, old boards, logs or rotting leaves
5. spray bottle for water
6. screening material

Directions for Making Habitat:

1. Place some small stones in the bottom of the container.
2. Place about eight to ten cm (5 inches) of a mixture of equal parts soil, sand and peat moss in the bottom of a large jar or aquarium.
3. Place rotting leaves and/or pieces of rotting log or bark on top of the soil.
4. Mist with water and repeat when dry.
5. Add wood lice (at least one per student, for use later) and keep in a shady place.
6. Cover with screening material.

Resources

Brillon, Gilles, Discovering Spiders, Snails, and Other Creepy Crawlers, Quintin Publishing, Quebec; ©1992
Hickman, Pamela, Habitats, Kids Can Press Ltd., Toronto ©1993
Pringle, Laurence, Discovering Nature Indoors, Doubleday and Company, Inc., ©1970

Name: _____

Student Tracking - Self-Evaluation

What is ↝⑥⑧↝❺☞✓	Activity 1	Activity 2	What Would You Like to Be?	'E' is for Ecology			
I completed this activity.							
I followed instructions carefully.							
I understood this activity.							
I listened to the ideas and suggestions of others.							
I worked diligently and did not waste time.							
I am proud of my work.							

The most important thing I learned was _____

_____

I think it is important to know this because _____

_____

A Habitat is a ❶⑥④↝✓	Activity 1	Backyard Investigation	Backyard Populations	Hunting for a Home			
I completed this activity.							
I followed instructions carefully.							
I understood this activity.							
I listened to the ideas and suggestions of others.							
I worked diligently and did not waste time.							
I am proud of my work.							

The most important thing I learned was _____

_____

I think it is important to know this because _____

_____

Name: _____

Student Tracking - Self-Evaluation

Food Chains ✓

	Activity 1	Activity 2	Activity 3	Making Food Cahins	How Do Plants Make Food?	Constructing Food Webs	Wolf Island	
I completed this activity.								
I followed instructions carefully.								
I understood this activity.								
I listened to the ideas and suggestions of others.								
I worked diligently and did not waste time.								
I am proud of my work.								

The most important thing I learned was _____

_____

I think it is important to know this because _____

_____

Each to Its

👋 👁️👁️👁️ ✓

	Activity 1	Activity 2	Watching Wood Lice	Wonderful Wood Lice				
I completed this activity.								
I followed instructions carefully.								
I understood this activity.								
I listened to the ideas and suggestions of others.								
I worked diligently and did not waste time.								
I am proud of my work.								

The most important thing I learned was _____

_____

I think it is important to know this because _____

_____

11

Name: _____

Student Tracking - Self-Evaluation

The Earth's Biomes ✓	Activity 1	Activity 2	Biome Mapping	Biome Research	Name That Biome	Drawing Landscapes		
I completed this activity.								
I followed instructions carefully.								
I understood this activity.								
I listened to the ideas and suggestions of others.								
I worked diligently and did not waste time.								
I am proud of my work.								

The most important thing I learned was _____

_____

I think it is important to know this because _____

_____

Adaptations ✓	Activity 1	Activity 2	A Perfect Match	Something's Fishy	Adapt an Animal		
I completed this activity.							
I followed instructions carefully.							
I understood this activity.							
I listened to the ideas and suggestions of others.							
I worked diligently and did not waste time.							
I am proud of my work.							

The most important thing I learned was _____

_____

I think it is important to know this because _____

_____

Name: _____

Student Tracking - Self-Evaluation

 Habitat Helpers ✓	Activity 1	Activity 2	Activity 3	Helping Habits	Endangered Species Report	Ecology Game	Let's Be Ecologists Speech	Crossword Wordsearch
I completed this activity.								
I followed instructions carefully.								
I understood this activity.								
I listened to the ideas and suggestions of others.								
I worked diligently and did not waste time.								
I am proud of my work.								

The most important thing I learned was _____

_____

I think it is important to know this because _____

_____

- -

Junior Ecologist
Award
presented to

_____

in recognition of outstanding achievement
in the study of

Habitats

Date: _____ Presented by: _____

Teacher Evaluation Sheet

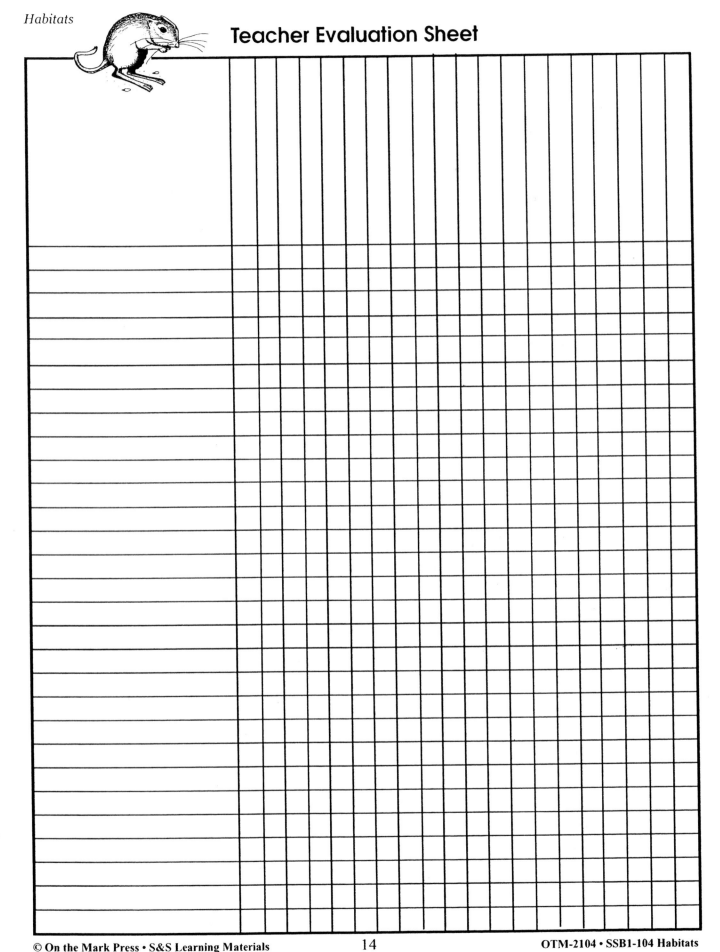

Name: _____

Teacher Observation Sheet

Name: _____

What is Ecology?

Vocabulary

1. _____
2. _____
3. _____
4. _____
5. _____
6. _____
7. _____
8. _____
9. _____
10. _____

5. _____
6. _____
7. _____
8. _____
9. _____

A Habitat is a Home

Food Chains Card 2

1. _____
2. _____
3. _____
4. _____
5. _____
6. _____
7. _____
8. _____

1. _____
2. _____
3. _____
4. _____
5. _____
6. _____
7. _____
8. _____

Each to Its Niche

Food Chains

1. _____
2. _____
3. _____
4. _____

1. _____
2. _____
3. _____
4. _____
5. _____
6. _____

Name: _____

The Earth's Biomes

Vocabulary
Cont'd

1. _____
2. _____
3. _____
4. _____
5. _____
6. _____
7. _____
8. _____
9. _____
10. _____
11. _____
12. _____
13. _____
14. _____
15. _____
16. _____
17. _____
18. _____

7. _____
8. _____
9. _____
10. _____

Habitat Helpers

1. _____
2. _____
3. _____
4. _____
5. _____
6. _____
7. _____
8. _____
9. _____
10. _____
11. _____
12. _____

Adaptations

1. _____
2. _____
3. _____
4. _____
5. _____
6. _____

Habitats

What is Ecology?

Overview

This component introduces students to the study of habitats as the science of ecology. The students will be invited to be **'Junior Ecologists.'** Children are naturally fascinated by living things and will take a keen interest in a study of plant and animal habitats. The book will be more meaningful to the students if live specimens are made available. This can be done easily by setting up one or more simple habitats in the classroom. The type of habitat and the choice of contents will make little difference to students. Many simple habitats can be set up with just a few simple materials and easily obtainable specimens. Students will enjoy and be very helpful in setting up habitats by finding the contents and maintaining them. Before setting up habitats, the students should understand that it is their responsibility as junior ecologists, to remove specimens carefully, to ensure that they are taken care of and to return them to their natural habitat at the end of the study. (See Setting Up Habitats, pp. 7-9)

Learning Expectations

Students will:

1. Understand that the information we have and continue to gain about plants and animals, their relationships to one another and their roles in the environment are due to the science of ecology.
2. Understand that the study of ecology is important to an understanding of environmental problems and possible solutions to those problems.
3. Understand that scientists gain information through observation and experimentation.
4. Have an understanding of the purpose of the activities to follow and approach them like young scientists.

Planning Ahead

1. Think about whether you will set up (a) simple habitat(s) ahead of time or make one with the assistance of the students. The students could help during the introductory lesson. (See Setting Up Classroom Habitats, pp. 7-9)
2. Gather interesting pictures, books, specimens and facts about plants and animals.
3. Locate a film, video or filmstrip about ecology.
4. Think about inviting an ecologist into the classroom to speak with the students.
5. Plan for the storage of student work, i.e. duo-tangs, folders etc. If making folders, the activity could be incorporated into the introductory lesson.
6. Make a chart of the vocabulary and post it in the room.
7. Find interesting facts about plants and animals that will spark interest.
8. Duplicate the student pages and make booklets.

Habitats

Implementation Suggestions

1. Use a display of interesting pictures and facts about plants and animals or the 'What is Ecology' information card as a springboard. Discuss how knowledge about plants and animals is collected and discuss its importance.

2. Discuss the term ecology and explain that an ecologist is a person who studies the relationships between plants and animals by studying natural habitats.

3. Invite the students to be junior ecologists, by introducing them to the mini-habitat in the classroom or discussing mini-habitats that they might set up on their own at home or cooperatively in the classroom. (See Habitats, by Pamela Hickman, for a wide variety of ideas) Explain that students will be responsible for observing and maintaining the habitat.

4. Allow the students time to look at and discuss the books and other materials in the classroom.

5. Cooperatively prepare a list of guidelines for obtaining materials for habitats, e.g. no trespassing, digging up full plant including root, checking conditions where found, etc.

6. Prepare a chart of rules for handling contents of mini-habitats, i.e. rules about washing hands after handling any material in the habitats and only handling, smelling or touching at appropriate times.

Resources

Cochrane, Jennifer, Plant Ecology; Wayland Publishers Ltd., London, ©1987
Cochrane, Jennifer, Urban Ecology; Wayland Publishers Ltd., London, ©1987
Hickman, Pamela, Habitats; Kids Can Press Ltd., Toronto, ©1993
MacDonald Educational Ltd., Exploring Ecology; Morrison and Gibb Ltd., London, ©1978
Pringle, Laurence, Discovering Nature Indoors, Doubleday And Company, Inc., ©1970
Twist, Clint, The Wayland Library of Science and Technology, Plants and Animals; Wayland Publishers, England, ©1990
Twist, Clint, The Wayland Library of Science and Technology, The Environment; Wayland Publishers, England, ©1990
Vancleave, Janice, Plants, John Wiley and Sons Inc., ©1997

Habitats

What is Ecology?

Do you like to read about plants and animals? Have you ever wondered where all the information about plants and animals comes from? Who collects all this information? Did you guess 'scientists?'

Scientists have been studying and collecting information about plants and animals for many years. There are many different types of scientists. An **ecologist** is a scientist who studies plants and animals as they are found in nature. Ecologists investigate the ways that plants and animals live together. The job of the ecologist is very important to keep our world healthy. As you learn about living things, perhaps you will understand why we should all be concerned with the study of plants and animals.

The reasons why plants and animals can be found living where they do is part of the science called **ecology**. The word ecology comes from two Greek words: **eco** comes from oikos which means house and **logy** comes from logos which means knowledge. Ecology is the study of the homes of plants and animals.

Many years ago, botanists (scientists who study plants) discovered that plants live in places to which they are suited. If a plant is placed in an area to which it is not suited it will probably die. For instance, a cactus would not grow well in the rain forest because the cactus needs hot sun and very little water. The cactus plant grows in the desert with other plants that are also suited to the heat and lack of rainfall. The desert has its own community of plants.

As botanists learned more and more, they found that plants are affected by the animals that live in the same area with the plants. They found that some plants do not grow well because they are eaten by animals before they are fully grown. Sometimes plants grow very well because they are not a source of food for animals. Other plants grow over large areas because the animals that share their space carry plant seeds far and wide. Botanists also found that animals are affected by the plants which grow in their community. Insects and animals live where the plants that they need for food grow. Some animals use plants, such as trees, for homes and protection.

Today, ecologists study communities of plants and animals and how they are linked together. They also study the effect humans have on plants and animals. When you have learned about how plants and animals survive, you will understand what humans can do to help preserve the many living things in our world.

What is Ecology?
Activity 1

Write these words in your vocabulary chart:

ecology	ecologist	investigate	botanist	suited
cactus	scientist	community	source	protection

Use the information card entitled 'What is Ecology?' to answer the following questions:

1. What is an ecologist?

    _____

    _____

2. A scientist who studies plants is called a _____ .

3. In a paragraph, explain how the science of ecology began.

    _____

    _____

    _____

    _____

    _____

    _____

    _____

    _____

    _____

    _____

4. Why do you think the job of the ecologist is more important today than ever?

    _____

    _____

    _____

    _____

    _____

    _____

    _____

    _____

What is Ecology?
Activity 2

1. **Using your dictionary, write the meaing of the word 'investigate.'**

   _____

   _____

2. Desert or dessert? Which of these words is 'tastier' than the other? Explain.

   _____

   _____

3. What does the word **'community'** mean?

   _____

   _____

4. Name four animals and a plant that each animal depends on to help it survive.

	Animal	Plant
Example:	koala	eucalyptus tree

5. An oak tree is a source of food and shelter for a squirrel. Think about your needs. List three needs and their source of supply for you.

Need	Source

What is Ecology?

What would you like to be?

> An ecologist is a person who studies plants and animals in their natural environment. Match the different sciences with what is studied and the person who specializes in that science.

A) meteorologist	a. meteorology	1. ____ the study of the earth's crust
B) _____	b. psychology	2. ____ the study of numbers
C) _____	c. seismology	3. ____ the study of living things
D) _____	d. technology	4. ____ the study of science in industry
E) _____	e. astrology	5. ____ the study of insects
F) _____	f. geology	6. ____ the study of earthquakes
G) _____	g. numerology	7. ____ the study of the mind
H) _____	h. biology	8. ____ the study of weather
I) _____	i. ornithology	9. ____ the study of stars and planets
J) _____	j. ichthyology	10. ____ the study of volcanoes
K) _____	k. paleontology	11. ____ the study of fossils
L) _____	l. anthropology	12. ____ the study of cosmetics
M) _____	m. volcanology	13. ____ the study of man
N) _____	n. cosmetology	14. ____ the study of fish
O) _____	o. entomology	15. ____ the study of birds

Skill: Word study, scientific terms, using the dictionary.

Name: _____

What is Ecology?

'E' is for Ecology!

There are many words associated with the study of ecology that begin with the letter 'e.' How many 'e' words can you find? Read the clues carefully.

1. everything around us _ _ _ _ _ _ _ _ _ _ _
2. the third planet from the sun _ _ _ _ _
3. a person who studies plants and animals _ _ _ _ _ _ _ _ _
4. a process in the water cycle _ _ _ _ _ _ _ _ _ _ _
5. a species that needs protection _ _ _ _ _ _ _ _ _ _
6. a living thing needs this to live _ _ _ _ _ _
7. a species that no longer exists _ _ _ _ _ _ _
8. a process which wears away the earth _ _ _ _ _ _ _
9. a large community of living things _ _ _ _ _ _ _ _ _
10. a coniferous tree _ _ _ _ _ _ _ _ _

Find the words that fit the blank spaces above in this worsearch puzzle.

```
F E R O S I O N Y B G R A E R
E N V I R O N M E N T E E W S
K P O E R F G H J L E L V B J
B H E E A R T H N G F K A F T
O J K C O P P E T H N H P H G
T E C O L O G I S T G F O D T
E N E R G Y E F E T U B R U B
E E E R G Y L I T A B G A S W
S X H G H Y E C O S Y S T E M
I T S W S T Y M O E O O I L I
H I N B G Y O G Y H K U O G T
E N D A N G E R E D S P N C I
G C A T U N C T H A E C O L Y
T T K N E W E J G P D E A N P
O E V E R G R E E N G Y G R E
```

Habitats
A Habitat is a Home
Overview

This component introduces the concept of habitat as a place which provides each living thing with what it needs to survive: food, water, shelter and space. The students will develop an awareness of living things and their habitats. Through an investigation of a backyard habitat, they will observe and record their observations using charts, maps and graphs.

Learning Expectations

Students will:

1. Identify, through observation, various factors that affect plants and animals in a specific habitat.
2. Recognize that animals and plants live in specific habitats because they are dependent on those habitats and have adapted to them.
3. Classify plants and animals observed in local habitats according to similarities and differences.
4. Formulate questions about and identify the needs of animals and plants in a particular habitat, and explore possible answers to these questions and ways of meeting these needs.
5. Plan investigations and identify variables that need to be held constant to ensure fair and accurate testing.
6. Use appropriate vocabulary and scientific terminology when describing investigations, explorations and observations. (e.g. habitat, population, community, etc.)
7. Compile data gathered through investigation, in order to record and present results using tally charts, tables and labeled graphs.

Planning Ahead

1. Locate as many plant, insect, tree, bird and flower guides as possible and ask the students, well in advance, to bring in any suitable books they may have at home.
2. Duplicate the student pages (Backyard Investigations pp. 29-31) and (Backyard Populations pp. 32-33).
3. Locate pictures, films, filmstrips etc. about birds, insects, trees, etc. for your area. (old calendars are a great source!) Students often have picture card collections of animals, birds, etc.
4. Make a chart of the vocabulary and post it in the room.
5. Invite a scientist such as an ornithologist, entomologist, etc. to visit the class.
6. Locate films, filmstrips and videos about habitats, backyard birds, insects, etc.
7. Write a letter to parents explaining briefly the (Backyard Investigation) assignment. (Optional)

Habitats

Implementation Suggestions

1. Use the picture book recommended, an appropriate film or the information card to introduce the topic.

2. Have the students think about their own habitats, how they provide them with the things they need for survival, and all the living things that share their habitats with them.

3. Discuss a backyard habitat, different small habitats that might be found there, and where they might be found.

4. The activities will need careful explanation and the children should be certain of your expectations. The graphing and mapping activities can be done separately depending on the abilities of the students. You might do a mapping lesson before asking the students to map the backyard area, and incorporate mapping skills such as symbols, legends, scale, etc. into the activity.

Resources

Book(s) recommended for introducing the component.

Cole, Joanna, <u>The Magic School Bus, Hops Home, A Book About Animal Habitats</u>, Scholastic Canada ©1995 (several titles in the (**Magic School Bus**) series are available on video)
Reed-Jones, Carol, <u>The Tree in the Ancient Forest</u>, Dawn Publications, Colorado, ©1995

Other useful books for implementing this topic:

Brillon, Gilles, <u>Discovering Spiders, Snails, and Other Creepy Crawlers</u>, Quintin Publishers, Quebec, ©1992
Burnie, David, <u>Forest</u>, Dorling Kindersley, ©1998
Hickman, Pamela, <u>Habitats</u>, Kids Can Press Ltd., Toronto, ©1993
Pfeffer, Wendy, <u>A Log's Life</u>, Simon and Schuster, New York, ©1997
Pringle, Laurence, <u>Discovering Nature Indoors</u>, Doubleday and Company, Inc., ©1970
Silver, Donald M., <u>One Small Square-Woods</u>, McGraw Hill, Canada, ©1995

Habitats

A Habitat is a Home

All living things depend on other living things for survival. Plants and animals that live in a particular place share the same water, air, climate and type of soil, which make up their physical environment. The plants and animals also share their physical environment with the other plants and animals living there. This is the biological environment. Both environments make up the habitat of each plant and animal.

Many plants and animals that use trees and sheltered areas for their homes live in a forest environment. Their environment is made up of the air, the water, the climate and the type of soil in the forest as well as the plants and animals living there. Birds, mice, owls, squirrels, deer and many other living things make their homes in the forest. Each plant and animal can be found living in a particular place that will supply it with the things it needs to survive: food, water, space and shelter. The particular place where each animal lives in the forest is called its habitat. Each plant or animal's habitat is made up of the climate, soil, air, water and other plants and animals that share its space.

In the forest there are many small habitats. Animals live in tree trunks, among dead leaves, in holes, in the branches of trees or under rocks. All of these places are habitats. Sometimes the habitats in the forest overlap. Animals may share the same space but they might make different use of that space.

Wood lice like to live under rocks or rotting logs where it is moist. The rotting log or rock is their habitat. They may share space with millipedes, moss and other living things. Together they all live in a community. They have associations with one another. This community is only one of the many communities of living things in the forest. The living things, along with the non-living things like soil, wind and rain form a very large habitat or what is called an ecosystem.

The plants and animals in the forest ecosystem affect each other in one way or another. They may compete with one another for food, eat each other or protect one another in some way. In a backyard habitat you might find robins, starlings, sparrows, squirrels, trees, plants, grass and insects among the many things living there. The robin may make its nest in the maple tree and feed on earthworms. Sparrows may live in the pine tree and eat insects or seeds from the bird feeder. Short plants may grow under the tall plants and vines may be growing on the fence. Moss may be growing on the trunks of trees. All these living things form a large backyard habitat which contains many smaller habitats.

Name: _____

A Habitat is a Home

Activity 1

Write these words in your vocabulary chart:

environment	**habitat**	**ecosystem**	**shelter**
survive	**climate**	**compete**	**soil**

1. Match each word with its meaning.

	environment	a	to try to win something
	survive	b	the lose top layer of the earth's surface
	shelter	c	the surroundings in which a plant or animal lives
	habitat	d	the place where a plant or animal usually lives
	climate	e	the plants and animals that live in balance with each other and the soils and climate around them
	soil	f	the usual weather a place has all year
	ecosystem	g	something that protects or covers
	compete	h	to stay alive

2. What four things are necessary for the survival of all living things?

   a) _____ b) _____ c) _____ d) _____

3. Explain how your habitat provides each of these things for you.

   a) _____
      _____

   b) _____
      _____

   c) _____
      _____

   d) _____

Name: _____

A Habitat is a Home

Backyard Investigation 1

For this investigation you will need to spend some time in your own or a friend's backyard. A backyard is home for many different plants and animals. You will need to be a good ecologist to observe and see connections between the plants and animals in the backyard habitat you are studying.

1. As you observe the living things you see, write them in the proper column of the chart.
2. If you don't know the name of a plant or animal, draw a small picture in one of the boxes on the chart.
3. Number each living thing and then write the number where you found it on your Backyard Investigation 2.

Plants	Trees	Birds	Insects	Animals

Skill: Classify plants and animals observed in local habitats.

Name: _____

A Habitat is a Home

Backyard Investigation 2

Look carefully as you study your backyard habitat. Choose an area around a tree to observe, as many living things can be found living in and around trees. A good ecologist observes plants and animals very carefully to determine how they use their habitat and share the space. As you discover each living thing, number it and write it in your backyard chart. Write the **number** of each living thing you have observed on the diagram below to show where you observed it.

Skill: Compile data gathered through investigation in order to record and present results, using tally charts, tables and graphs.

A Habitat is a Home

Backyard Investigation 3

Draw a map of the 'backyard habitat' you investigated as though you were looking down from a helicopter.

Skill: Mapping, creating a sketch map of a familiar place.

Name: _____

A Habitat is a Home

Backyard Populations

Activity 1

Through your investigation you found a wide variety of plants and animals in your backyard habitat. Perhaps you counted three robins, six sparrows, three squirrels, twelve dandelions, etc. Your backyard area therefore has a 'population' of robins, a population of sparrows and a population of squirrels, etc. There might also have been a population of maple trees, one of grass and another of dandelions.

If you listed every population you would probably have a very long list. The list would include the number of populations of insects, of birds, of mammals, of trees, of plants, of spiders, etc. The total number of populations equals the number of different species of plants and animals living in the backyard habitat.

Look carefully at the data you collected from your backyard investigation. Use your data to make a graph of the number of populations of insects, trees, plants, birds, mammals and any other populations you feel should be included.

For example, if you found six different species of insects, you would show six in the insect column. If you observed four species of birds, you would show four in the bird column.

When you have completed your graph, answer the following questions:

1. How many populations of birds did you observe? _____

2. How many different species of insects did you observe? _____

3. Did you notice any similarities or differences about the habitats of the insects in your investigation? _____

   _____

   _____

   _____

4. What was the most interesting part of your investigation?

   _____

   _____

   _____

   _____

   _____

Skill: Understanding the concept of population in ecology; gathering and displaying data collected on a labeled graph.

A Habitat is a Home

Backyard Populations

Activity 2

Make a bar graph of the number of populations of living things you found in the backyard area you investigated. Label each axis. Color your graph neatly and give it a title.

Skill: Constructing and displaying data collected on a labeled graph.

Name: _____

A Habitat is a Home

Hunting for a Home

You may have to do some research to fill in the blanks with the name of plants or animals.

1. A cave is a home for a _____, _____, _____.

2. A nest is a home for a _____, _____, _____.

3. A den is a home for a _____, _____, _____.

4. A backyard is a home for a _____, _____, _____.

5. A rotting log is home to a _____, _____, _____.

6. A shell is a home for a _____, _____, _____.

7. A pond is a home for a _____, _____, _____.

8. A mountain is home to a _____, _____, _____.

9. A forest is a home for a _____, _____, _____.

10. An ocean is a home for a _____, _____, _____.

11. A tree is a home for a _____, _____, _____.

12. A swamp is home to a _____, _____, _____.

13. A burrow is home to a _____, _____, _____.

14. The Canadian Praries is home to a _____, _____, _____.

15. The American Desert is home to a _____, _____, _____.

16. The Arctic is home to a _____, _____, _____.

17. The African Savannah is home to a _____, _____, _____.

18. The Canadian Tundra is home to a _____, _____, _____.

19. The South American rainforest is home to a _____, _____, _____.

20. The Arabian Desert is home to a _____, _____, _____.

Habitats
Food Chains
Overview

This component introduces the students to food chains. It involves concepts related to energy, plant growth and producers and consumers. They will learn that all energy comes from the sun and that every living thing is part of one or more food chains. This component lends itself to plant activities. There are numerous good books available.

Learning Expectations

Students will:

1. Demonstrate an understanding of a food chain as a system in which energy from the sun is eventually transferred to animals.
2. Classify organisms according to their roles in a food chain.
3. Construct food chains of different plant and animal species as well as humans.
4. Classify animals as herbivore, carnivore, omnivore and insectivore.
5. Understand that the extinction of a plant or animal species affects the rest of the natural community.
6. Investigate ways in which the extinction of a plant or animal species affects the rest of the natural community and humans.
7. Use appropriate vocabulary and scientific terminology when describing investigations, explorations and observations.
8. Show the effects on plants and animals of the loss of their natural habitats.

Planning Ahead

1. Locate the book **Wolf Island** by Celia Godkin to be used with the student activity on page 47.
2. Locate reference books about wolves that might interest some students in doing some quick research.
3. Duplicate the student pages and make a booklet.
4. Locate films or filmstrips about food chains, plants and energy.
5. Make a chart of the vocabulary words and post it in the room.
6. Collect different types of plants for display in the classroom.
7. Set up a few simple plant demonstrations such as a celery stick or carnation in water to which food coloring has been added, beans for sprouting, cuttings in water, cacti, etc.
8. Make a display of books about plants and simple plant experiments that the students can read and think about, trying either at school or at home.
9. Locate any plant and animal specimens such as teeth, claws, different types of seeds, preserved specimens, etc. Check with the Science department at your school. They usually have plant and animal specimens in jars. Make certain the specimens are preserved in substances that would not be harmful to children and which are preferably stored in plastic jars.

Habitats

Implementation Suggestions

1. Use an appropriate film, the recommended book or the information card to introduce the topic. (A film could be about energy, plants or food chains.)

2. Discuss 'energy.' What is it? Why do we need it? Where do we get it?

3. Using a display of animal pictures, have students classify them as herbivore, omnivore, carnivore or insectivore.

4. Discuss the term 'food chain' and explain that every living thing is part of a food chain. Have students work as a group to plan one meal. After they have planned the meal, have them make a chart of the food chains for each food to present to the class.

5. Read the story '**Wolf Island**,' discuss it and have students complete the activity page 'Wolf Island.'

6. Have students write their own story about an ecosystem where one important member of the food web was eliminated. They could model their story on 'Wolf Island.'

Resources

Book(s) recommended for introducing the component:

Cole, Joanna, <u>The Magic School Bus Gets Eaten, A Book About Deserts</u>, Scholastic Canada ©1995 (several titles in the "**Magic School Bus**" series are available on video)

Other useful books for implementing this topic:

Ganeri, Anita, <u>The Hunt For Food</u>, Belitha Press Ltd., London, ©1994
Godkin, Celia, <u>Wolf Island</u>, Fitzhenry Whiteside, Toronto, ©1995 (needed for page 47 student activity)
Lauber, Patricia, <u>Who Eats What? Food Chains and Food Webs</u>, Harper Collins, ©1995
S&S Learning Materials, <u>Wolf Island</u>, Novel Study SSN1-213, Napanee, ©2000

Food Chains

Information Card 1

All living things need energy to grow. Without energy, you and all other living things would not survive. You need energy to grow and do all the things you do. What is energy? Where do all living things get the energy they need?

All energy comes from the sun in the form of heat and light. The only living things that can trap the sun's energy are plants. Plants store energy for us and all other living things to use. It is easy to see that plants are the most important living things on our planet. Without plants, there wouldn't be any life on Earth.

You get the energy you need to survive from the food you eat. Everything you eat started with energy from the sun which was trapped by plants. You get some of your energy directly from plants and some from animals which have eaten plants.

The energy from plants is passed to all other living things through food chains. Everything you eat is part of a food chain. Plants are called **primary producers** because they trap the sun's energy and use it first. Some animals called **herbivores** eat only plants. The energy from the plants is passed on to the herbivores who eat them. The herbivores are called **primary consumers** because they get energy directly from the plants. A rabbit is a primary consumer because it is a herbivore. It eats only plants. When a rabbit eats a plant, the energy in the plant is passed on to the rabbit. This energy helps the rabbit grow, run about and reproduce. When the rabbit is caught and eaten by an owl or other predators, the energy that is contained in the rabbit is then passed on to the owl. The owl doesn't have any predators, so it is at the end of the food chain.

Animals like the owl, that eat herbivores, are called **secondary consumers**. They are also called **carnivores**. Carnivores are animals that eat only meat. Carnivores often eat other carnivores, and so we can see that the energy that started with the sun is passed from one living thing to another through food chains.

Most humans eat both plants and animals, so they are called '**omnivores**'. Think about some of your favorite animals. Are they herbivores, carnivores or omnivores? What do you think an **insectivore** is?

Name: _____

Food Chains

Activity 1

Write these words in your vocabulary chart:

carnivore	secondary consumer	energy
omnivore	producer	predator
herbivore	primary consumer	insectivore

1. Write **T** for True or **F** for False for each of the following sentences.

   _____ a) Only humans need energy to survive.

   _____ b) There wouldn't be any life on Earth without plants.

   _____ c) Humans get energy directly from the sun.

   _____ d) All living things can trap the sun's energy.

   _____ e) Plants are called primary consumers.

   _____ f) Plants pass on energy through food chains.

   _____ g) An owl is a secondary producer.

   _____ h) Herbivores are primary consumers.

   _____ i) Animals that eat herbivores are secondary consumers.

   _____ j) Carnivores eat plants and animals.

2. Write a definition for each of the following words:

   a) carnivore _____

   b) omnivore _____

   c) herbivore _____

Skill: Classify animals according to their roles in the food chain; classify animals as herbivore, carnivore, omnivore.

Name: _____

Food Chains
Activity 2

1. Place the following living things in the correct place in the chart:

owl	hawk	human	robin	frog
deer	worm	rabbit	anteater	grasshopper
bear	seal	moose	skunk	baboon

Herbivore	Carnivore	Omnivore	Insectivore

2. What is 'predator?'

_____

_____

_____

3. What is 'prey?'

_____

_____

_____

Skill: Classify animals according to their roles in the food chain; classify animals as herbivore, carnivore, omnivore.

Food Chains
Activity 3

Fill in the blanks with these words:

energy	producers	consumers	heat	light
sun	leaves	roots	food	
food chains	fruit	stems	seeds	

Producers and Consumers

At the beginning of every food chain is the _____. All living things need energy to survive. They obtain energy directly or indirectly from the sun. The sun provides energy in the form of _____ and _____. Without the sun, nothing could survive.

Plants need _____ from the sun to grow. Plants are called _____ because they produce materials that can be eaten by other living things. Some part of the plants that are consumed are: _____, _____, _____, _____ and _____.

All living things depend on other living things for _____. Animals and humans eat or consume plants to gain energy and are called _____. Plants, animals and humans are all part of _____ _____.

Skill: Understand that a food chain is a system in which energy from the sun is eventually transferred to animals.

Food Chains

Making Food Chains

Name: _____

Make your own food chains by drawing a picture in each box and writing the name of the plant or animal on the line below the box.

Skill: Understand that food chains are systems in which energy from the sun is eventually transferred to animals.

Food Chains
How Do Plants Make Food?

Information Card 2

To make food, plants need water from the soil and **carbon dioxide** from the air. They trap energy from the sun in the form of heat and light and change it into food called **glucose**. Plants can only make food if they have sunlight.

The sun helps the plants turn water and **carbon dioxide** into glucose through a process called '**photosynthesis**.' Photosynthesis means making food with light. Photosynthesis can only take place in plants which contain a green substance called **chlorophyll**. Chlorophyll is the substance which makes a plant's leaves green. Sunlight falls on the green leaves of the plant and is absorbed with the help of chlorophyll.

When plants make food they produce **oxygen**. Oxygen is the gas in the air and water that all living things need to live. Plants produce more oxygen than they need and so they give off the extra oxygen into the air. This oxygen helps to replace the oxygen that is used by all living things as they breathe.

Plants cannot make food from water and carbon dioxide only. They need other nutrients which they get from the soil. When water is added to the soil, the nutrients in the soil are carried into the plant through little hairs on the roots of the plant.

Name: _____

Food Chains

How Do Plants Make Food?
Activity 1

Write these words in your vocabulary chart:

carbon dioxide	oxygen	absorbed	nutrients
photosynthesis	chlorophyll	substance	glucose

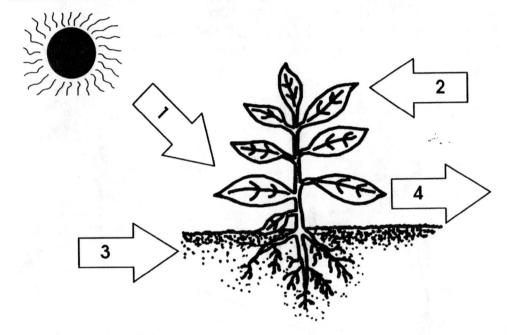

Read Food Chains *Information Card 2.*

Explain what is happening at each arrow.

1. _____

   _____

2. _____

   _____

3. _____

   _____

4. _____

   _____

Skill: Understanding that a food chain is a system in which energy from the sun is eventually transferred to animals.

Food Chains

Food Webs

Information Card 3

The sun is the source of all food and energy. When ecologists study food chains, they can see how energy is passed from one living thing to another in an **ecosystem**.

Some food chains are very short, because some animals will only eat one kind of food. For example, the panda eats only bamboo shoots. Most animals, however, eat more than one kind of food, and so they belong to many food chains.

In the forest ecosystem, food chains are very complicated. The rabbit eats many different kinds of plants. The fox may eat the rabbit, but it also eats insects, birds, worms and other small animals. When food chains start to become very complex they are called 'food webs.'

A food Web might look something like this:

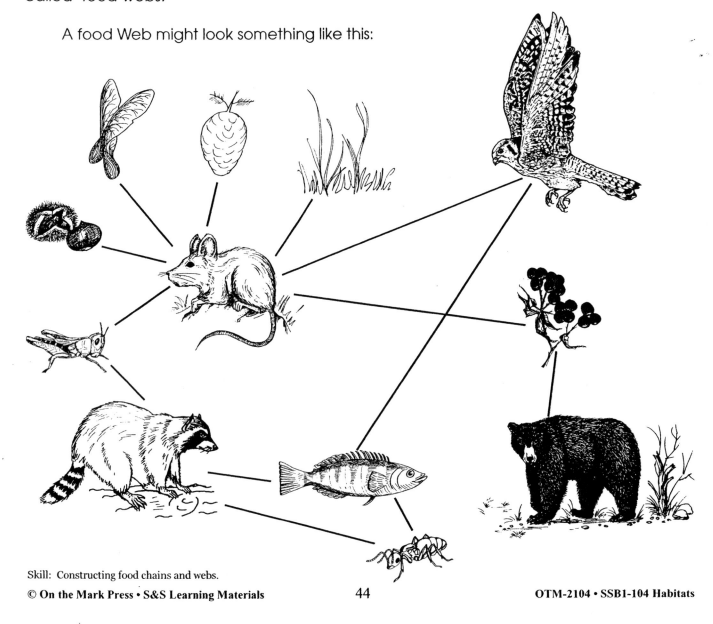

Skill: Constructing food chains and webs.

Name: _____

Food Chains
Constructing Food Webs
Activity 1

Read and follow the instructions carefully:

1. Read Food Chains *Information Card 3*.
2. Cut apart the Food Web Cards
3. Use as many cards as you wish to make a food web.
4. Use the blank cards to draw your own pictures.
5. Glue the cards onto 'Constructing Food Web' Activity 2.
6. Connect the pictures with arrows.

Food Web Cards

BEETLES	MICE	FISH	OWLS	INSECTS
BIRDS	ACORNS	SKUNKS	RABBITS	BEARS
SQUIRRELS	FROGS	COYOTES	SUN	RACCOONS
WATER PLANTS	GRAINS	SPIDERS	GRASSES	NUTS - SEEDS
BERRIES				

Skill: Constructing food chains and webs.

Habitats

Name: _____

Food Chains
Constructing Food Webs
Activity 2

Skill: Constructing food chains and webs.

© On the Mark Press • S&S Learning Materials   46   OTM-2104 • SSB1-104 Habitats

Name: _____

Food Chains

Wolf Island

After you have read or heard the story **Wolf Island** by Celia Godkin, complete this activity.

1. List six animals that live on Wolf Island:

   1. _____   4. _____

   2. _____   5. _____

   3. _____   6. _____

2. Draw a food web showing how the animals on Wolf Island lived in balance with one another. Use arrows to connect your pictures.

3. Explain what happened to the island ecosystem when the wolves left.

   _____

   _____

   _____

   _____

   _____

   _____

   _____

Skill: Investigate ways in which the extinction of an animal affects the rest of the natural environment.

Habitats

Each to Its Niche

Overview

This component involves the students' participation in an investigation of **wood lice**, commonly knows as pill bugs or sow bugs. They are interesting creatures and perform an important role as decomposers. Without decomposers such as millipedes, mites, bacteria, earthworms, fungi, etc., the world would be littered with garbage. This investigation has two separate activities involving wood lice. If you set up the wood lice habitat in the classroom, you will have them readily available. If you chose not to set up the habitat, then have each student bring in one or two wood lice for the activities. They can easily be found under rocks and logs in the garden or other damp places. The students should be reminded to transport them in a plastic container, like a pill bottle, with some moist leaves, etc. The wood lice should be returned to their habitat after the investigation, or the students could set up one large habitat.

Learning Expectations

Students will:

1. Identify, through observation, various factors that affect plants and animals in a specific habitat.
2. Describe the structural adaptations of plants and animals that demonstrate a response of living things to their environment.
3. Recognize that animals and plants live in specific habitats because they are dependent on those habitats and have adapted to them.
4. Formulate questions about and identify the needs of animals and plants in a particular habitat; explore possible answers to these questions and ways of meeting these needs.
5. Plan investigations and identify variables that need to be held constant to ensure fair and accurate testing.
6. Use appropriate vocabulary and science terminology when describing investigations, explorations and observations.
7. Compile data gathered through investigation, in order to record and present results, using tally charts, tables and labeled graphs.
8. Communicate the procedures and results of investigations.

Planning Ahead

1. Set up wood lice (pill bugs) habitat.
2. Duplicate the student activity pages and make booklets.
3. Collect magnifying glasses and magnifying boxes.
4. Locate films and filmstrips about the formation of soil, earthworms, etc.
5. Plan a procedure for hand washing during science investigations.

  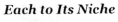 

Habitats

Implementation Suggestions

1. Use the information card or recommended picture book to introduce the term **ecological niche** as the role of every living thing in its community of living things. An analogy could be made to the school community. The students could identify the roles of the different people in the school community and how the school would not function smoothly without each person doing his/her job.

2. Show the students a sample of soil and discuss how soil is formed. How do leaves and other dead plants and animals decompose? Explain the term **decompose** and why wood lice are known as decomposers.

3. Introduce the students to the wood lice and their role in the living community of things to which they belong. Discuss where the wood lice are found and explain that as junior ecologists, they will observe and make notes about the wood lice.

4. Explain the scientific method of investigation and its importance to the job of the scientist.

Resources

Book(s) recommended for introducing the component:

Pfeffer, Wendy, <u>A Log's Life</u>, Simon and Schuster, New York, ©1997

Other useful books for implementing this topic:

Brillon, Gilles, <u>Discovering Spiders, Snails, and Other Creepy Crawlers</u>, Quintin Publishers, Quebec, ©1992
Burnie, David, <u>Forest</u>, Dorling Kindersley, ©1998
Hickman, Pamela, <u>Habitats</u>, Kids Can Press Ltd., Toronto, ©1993
Pringle, Laurence, <u>Discovering Nature Indoors</u>, Doubleday And Company, ©1970
Reed-Jones, Carol, <u>The Tree in the Ancient Forest</u>, Dawn Publications, Colorado, ©1995
Silver, Donald M., <u>One Small Square - Woods</u>, McGraw Hill, Canada, ©1995

Habitats

Information About Wood Lice

Wood Lice:

- are also know as sow bugs; one type of sow bug, when startled, will roll itself into a ball, and is known as a pill bug

- have gills and need a moist environment

- will roll up in a ball for protection whereas some sow bugs, which are very similar, will not

- are members of the family called 'crustaceans;' other members of this family include lobsters and crayfish

- survive on dead plant material

- like to hide in moist, dark places, often under wood in fields, forests, damp basements, etc.

- use their antennae to touch and smell; they have seven pairs of legs

- have white folds on their underside (gills) which they use for breathing - require a high level of humidity

- reproduce by laying eggs

- molt as they grow, which means to shed their outer skin

- chew up rotting material which can then be broken down by bacteria into nutrients for plants

- can be caught with a raw potato trap (cut potato in half, scoop out some of the inside, turn potato over on moist area and make certain there is an entrance)

- like to eat moist paper or potato

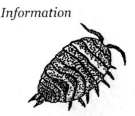

Habitats
Each to Its Niche

The plants and animals found in an ecosystem make up the living community of that area. The kind of place where a particular plant or animal lives in the community is its habitat. There are many kinds of habitats and the living things found in those habitats all have their own part to play in the community of living things in which they live.

All plants and animals will grow and thrive in a place which meet all their needs. A plant or animal may have enemies in its environment. It may also be a threat to other plants and animals, but it has adapted to life in its environment and is able to survive there. In your community, different people have different jobs to do. Everyone is important to the smooth functioning of the community. If everyone in the community did the same job, there wouldn't be enough work for everyone or enough customers. Some people would have to do different jobs or move away. In the same way, all the plants and animals in a community have their own jobs or way of life. The job of plants is to make their own food so that they can grow and reproduce and be a source of food for animals. Animals cannot make their own food, and so their job is to eat plants or other animals to survive and reproduce. Some animals eat other animals and some eat plants or parts of plants, like seeds and nuts. Bees pollinate flowers. Squirrels bury nuts and seeds. Earthworms help to break up the soil. Wood lice eat rotting leaves and plants and break this material into smaller bits. Baceria breaks these smaller bits into nutrients that plants can use. Every living thing has its own job.

No two species of animals can survive in the community very long, as they would have to compete with one another for water, food, space and shelter. One of the species would have to move away or die.

Each plant or animal is affected by or affects the other living things in its environment. The job or way of life of each living thing is called its 'ecological niche.' In an ecosystem all the plants and animals depend on each other to do their jobs so that the ecosystem will work efficiently. All living things, along with the soil, air and water that make up their habitats, must work together. If one part of the ecosystem changes suddenly, then the whole ecosystem and the living things in it will be affected in some way. Then the system will not be in a state of balance.

Name: _____

Each to Its Niche

Activity 1

Write these words in your vocabulary chart:

ecological niche	balance	reproduce
species	thrive	adapted

1. Explain the term "ecological niche".

   _____

   _____

   _____

2. What is the ecological niche of each of the following animals?

   a) deer _____

   _____

   b) earthworm _____

   _____

   c) wood lice _____

   _____

   d) squirrel _____

   _____

   e) robin _____

   _____

   f) hawk _____

   _____

   g) grey wolf _____

   _____

Name: _____

Each to Its Niche

Activity 2

Think about an ecosystem near your home. Explain how the living things in that ecosystem work together to keep the ecosystem in balance.

_____

_____

_____

_____

_____

_____

_____

_____

_____

_____

_____

_____

Choose a plant or animal from the ecosystem and tell what would happen if that plant or animal were removed from the ecosystem.

_____

_____

_____

_____

_____

_____

_____

_____

_____

_____

_____

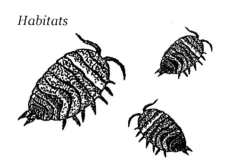

Each to Its Niche

Watching Wood Lice

Activity 1

If you look under a rock, log, or old leaves in your garden, you will most probably find some interesting little bugs called 'wood lice.' Wood lice like to live in dark, moist places. Wood lice are also called sow bugs or pill bugs.

Wood lice are members of a community of living things called decomposers. **Decomposers** have a very important job. They help to break down large pieces of **rotting plants into tiny pieces that can be eaten by other small animals called bacteria** and **fungi**. The bacteria and fungi change the pieces left by the wood lice into nutrients which can then be used by plants. Perhaps you will do a little research and find out more about decomposers.

As you observe your wood lice, try to find answers to these questions:

1. What do wood lice do when you pick them up? Do they all react the same? If not, perhaps you have pill bugs and sow bugs. Can you tell the difference between them?

2. How do they breathe under rocks and logs, etc.?

3. The pill bug's scientific name is **armadillidium.** Can you think of an animal whose name sounds like that? Does the pill bug resemble this animal?

4. How many legs do wood lice have?

5. Wood lice molt. Can you see any evidence of this?

6. Wood lice are closely related to crayfish and lobsters. Can you tell why?

7. What animal family do crayfish, lobsters and wood lice belong to?

8. Do some research to learn more about bacteria and fungi.

Name: _____

Each to Its Niche

Watching Wood Lice

Activity 2

After observing the wood lice, and before returning them to their habitat, draw a detailed diagram of one wood louse.

1. Write down what you have learned about wood lice through your observations.

   _____

   _____

   _____

   _____

   _____

2. What other things would you like to know about wood lice?

   _____

   _____

   _____

   _____

   _____

Skill: Formulating questions about, identifying and exploring the needs of animals in a particular habitat.

Name: _____

Each to Its Niche

Wonderful Wood Lice

Scientific Investigation 1

Wood lice are closely related to lobsters and crayfish. Wood lice live on land, but they breathe through gills as fish do. Wood lice live in damp areas to stay moist because their gills work only when they're wet.

> **Since wood lice need a moist habitat to survive, they must be experts at finding water.**

1. Do you think the sentence in the box could be true?
2. With a partner, plan an experiment to find out.
3. List the materials you will need.

Use the space below to plan your investigation.

This is what we plan to do:

_____
_____
_____
_____
_____
_____
_____
_____
_____
_____
_____

Materials we will need:

_____
_____
_____

Skill: Recognize that animals live in specific habitats because they are dependent on those habitats and have adapted to them.

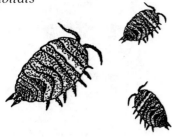

Name: _____

Each to Its Niche

Wonderful Wood Lice

Scientific Investigation 2

Purpose: We wonder what will happen if...

_____

_____

_____

Hypothesis: What we think will happen is...

_____

_____

_____

Procedure: The steps we used were...

_____

_____

_____

_____

_____

_____

Observation: We observed the following...

_____

_____

_____

_____

_____

_____

Conclusion: We learned that...

_____

_____

_____

_____

_____

_____

Skill: Formulating questions about, identifying and exploring the needs of animals in a particular habitat.

Habitats
The Earth's Biomes
Overview

This component introduces the students to the major biomes throughout the world. There are over thirty different biomes, however this book will only look at the largest and most common biomes: the polar regions, the deciduous forests, the coniferous forests, the deserts, the grasslands, the mountain regions, the tundra, the rainforest and the water biomes (oceans, freshwater lakes, streams and ponds, and wetlands areas such as bogs, swamps and marshes.) Students will examine the plant and animal life in each region.

Learning Expectations

Students will:

1. Identify, through observation, various factors that affect plants and animals in a specific habitat.
2. Describe the structural adaptations of plants and animals that demonstrate a response of living things to their environment.
3. Recognize that animals and plants live in specific habitats because they are dependent on those habitats and have adapted to them.
4. Formulate questions about and identify the needs of animals and plants in a particular habitat, and explore possible answers to these questions and ways of meeting these needs.
5. Plan investigations and identify variables that need to be held constant to ensure fair and accurate testing.
6. Construct food chains that include different plant and animal species.
7. Show the effects on plants and animals of the loss of their natural habitat.

Planning Ahead

1. Locate as many pictures, videos, filmstrips, etc. about the different biomes as possible.
2. Locate books about the desert, forest, wetlands, polar regions, etc.
3. Make a chart of the vocabulary and post it in the room.
4. If using the research activity, plan some lessons about how to do research, and perhaps make arrangements with your librarian for a lesson.
5. Locate or make a map of the world that can be used for reference when investigating the biomes.
6. Arrange to have atlases available for students to use during their research times.
7. Make a bulletin board with pictures of the different biomes and the plant and animal life found in each.
8. Obtain plant and animal specimens such as cacti, pine cones and needles, fur, etc.
9. Duplicate the student pages.

Habitats

Implementation Suggestions

1. Use the recommended book, information card, or film to introduce the topic.

2. A film or video about the Arctic, the desert, the prairies, etc. would be a good introduction.

3. Using a map of the world, discuss the climate of the different regions of the world and try to determine what the students already know about the biomes of the world.

4. Make a list, with the students, of all the things they would like to learn about the different biomes and the plants and animals found in each.

5. Allow students ample time to study the materials available in the room.

6. Make good use of the many excellent videos, films, etc. available.

Resources

Book(s) recommended for introducing the component:

Kalman, Bobbie, <u>What is a Biome?</u>, Crabtree Publishing Co., Canada, ©1998

Other useful books for implementing this topic:

MacDonald Educational Ltd., <u>Exploring Ecology</u>, Morrison and Gibb Ltd., London, ©1978 (**Note:** Books about the different regions of the world are far too numerous to list and most libraries are well stocked.)

Habitats

The Earth's Biomes

Ecologists divide our planet into large areas that have the same type of vegetation and climate. We describe the climate of a region by its temperature, rainfall, wind and the amount of light it receives. The **vegetation** is the plant life that we find growing in the region. We call these large regions of the earth **biomes**. Biomes can be compared to very large ecosystems. Scientists sometimes disagree on the number of biomes on the earth but there are more than thirty. You should be familiar with only the major biomes of the earth. They are the forests, grasslands, deserts, mountains, tundra, polar regions and the three water biomes of the planet.

Only plants and animals that are suited to a region will grow and live there. Where there is a hot, dry climate we have **deserts**. For example in the desert, only plants and animals that can live with the heat and lack of rainfall can survive. There are many kinds of deserts. Deserts get very little precipitation and are hot all year.

Forests form another major biome of our planet. There are many types of forests. Each has its own climate, plants and animals. Near the equator, where it is always very hot and rainy, we find areas of thick tropical forests called **rainforests**. Rainforests develop where the temperature is always above 18° C (66° F) and the rainfall is around 200 cm (70 inches.) These areas are very hot and humid because of the great amounts of water in the air. The temperature doesn't change much, and in some rainforests it rains everyday. Rainforests have very thick vegetation and most of the trees have broad leaves.

Most of the forests which cover North America, Europe and Asia are **coniferous** and **deciduous** forests. In a coniferous forest, conifers (trees with needles) are most common. These trees get their name from the fact that they grow cones which are filled with seeds. Many animals of a coniferous forest feed on these cones. There are many different types of coniferous forests throughout the world. The type of trees growing in each forest depends on the climate of the region. Deciduous forests have trees with broad leaves that fall in autumn. Examples of deciduous trees are maple, oak, birch and poplar.

Some of the earth's large biomes are **grasslands**. These are large, flat or gently rolling areas covered with grass. There are many types of grasslands around the world, all with their own kinds of weather. The grasslands in the cool regions of the world are called **temperate** grasslands. Temperate grasslands have few trees because there is not enough rain. They receive 25-50 cm (10-20 inches) per year. In North America they are called **prairies** or plains. The grasslands in the middle of Eurasia are called **steppes**. In the middle of the large southern continents, where it is very hot, the grasslands are called **savannas** or **tropical** grasslands. The savanna is covered in bushes and tough grasses. There are few trees because most of the year there is little rain. The grassland area of

Habitats
The Earth's Biomes

South America is called the **pampas**. It receives very little rainfall and is very dry due to its cold, dry winds.

The top and bottom of the world where there is always snow and ice are the polar regions. The climate is always icy cold and there is no vegetation. The animals living there depend mostly on ocean plants and other animals for their food.

Just below the polar regions is the **tundra**. The tundra is a huge treeless plain which reaches from the Arctic Ocean to the northern forests. Most of the year it is windy and freezing cold. The water and land are frozen. Trees will not grow in this area of the world because the earth is permanently frozen. Only when the land thaws a little in the summer can grasses and small shrubs grow. During the summer season, a thin layer of the frozen soil melts and some plant life begins to grow. Plants such as mosses, lichens and grasses grow and provide food for much of the tundra wildlife.

The mountain regions of the world contain a wide variety of plant life and vegetation because of the differing altitudes at the bottoms and tops of the mountains. At lower altitudes there may be tropical forests and plants. As the altitude increases the plant and animal life changes, sometimes from deciduous to coniferous to mosses and lichens. Traveling up a mountain is like traveling through many different biomes.

Ecologists also divide the waters of the earth into three biomes. These are the oceans, which are salty, and the fresh waters like lakes, rivers, streams and ponds, which are not salty. Bogs, swamps and marshes are called **wetland** biomes. In these areas the soil contains a great deal of water. Freshwater biomes are found all over the world and provide habitats for many plants and animals.

Name: _____

The Earth's Biomes

Activity 1

Write these words in your vocabulary chart:

biome	coniferous	pampas	tundra	temperature
vegetation	deciduous	prairies	altitude	precipitation
tropical	rainforest	plains	wetland	humid
polar	savanna	steppe		

1. What is a biome? _____

    _____

2. List four things that are used to determine the climate of an area.

    a) _____ b) _____ c) _____ d) _____

3. Two words that can be used instead of the word 'vegetation' are

    _____ _____

4. In what type of forest would you find a pine tree? _____

5. The deciduous forest contains mostly trees with _____ _____.

6. How much precipitation does a forest have to receive to be called a rainforest?

    _____

7. Two kinds of precipitation are _____ and _____.

8. What do we call the grasslands found in Canada? _____

    the United States? _____

    Africa? _____

    South America? _____

    Eurasia? _____

Skill: Recognizing that plants live in specific habitats because they are dependent on those habitats and have adapted to them.

Name: _____

The Earth's Biomes

Activity 2

1. Choose the words that best describe the vegetation of each biome.

mosses and lichen
treeless
evergreens
maple, oaks, populars, etc.

tough grasses, few trees
thick plant growth
cacti or palms

Tropical Grassland	
Desert	
Coniferous Forest	
Tundra	
Polar Region	
Rainforest	
Deciduous Forest	

2. Three water biomes are _____, _____, and

_____.

3. Fill in the chart with names of trees.

Coniferous Trees	Deciduous Trees

Skill: Recognizing that plants and animals live in specific habitats because they are dependent on those habitats and have adapted to them.

Habitats
The Earth's Biomes

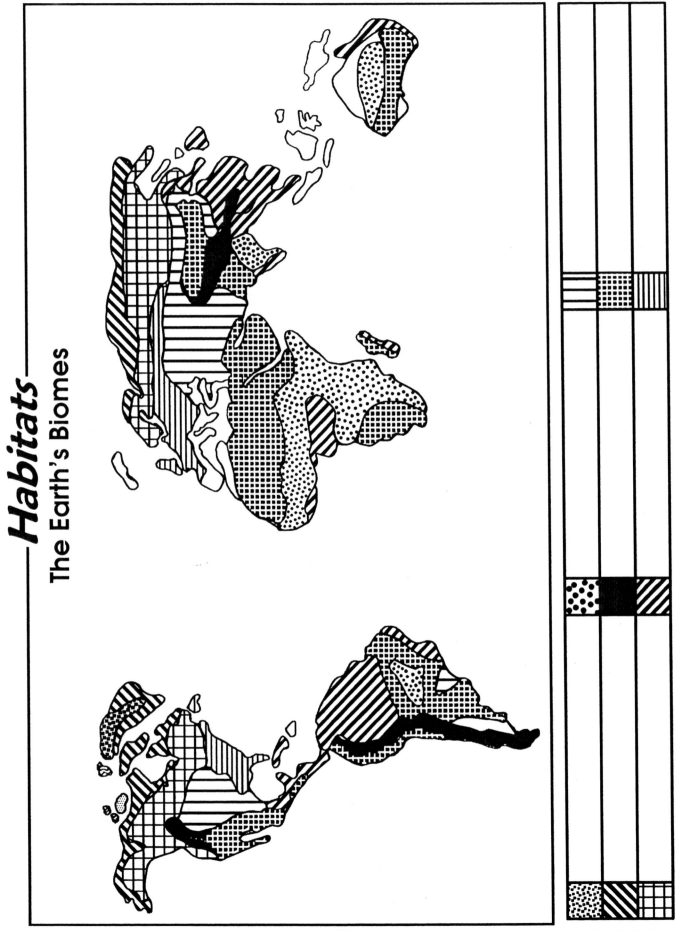

Name: _____

The Earth's Biomes

Mapping Activity

You will need a copy of the map titled 'The Earth's Biomes' for this activity.

1. Complete the legend on the map by studying the map and using an atlas or other reference materials. Books about ecology often have maps of the biomes of the world. The following is a list of the nine biomes you should use in your legend:

   1) Polar Regions
   2) Tundra
   3) Tropical Forests
   4) Tropical Grasslands
   5) Temperate Grasslands
   6) Deserts and Semi-Deserts
   7) Mountains
   8) Coniferous Forests
   9) Deciduous Forests

2. The two biomes which make up most of the continent of Africa are _____ _____ and _____.

3. The biome which covers most of the country in which I live is _____.

4. The largest biome of the earth, not shown in the legend, is _____.

5. The two largest biomes of Australia are _____ and _____.

6. The tundra biomes are located only in the _____ hemisphere.

7. Tropical forests are located near the _____.

8. Most of Central America is a _____ biome.

9. The temperate grassland biomes are found on the continents of _____ and _____.

Name: _____

Biome Research 1

_____

Location

_____
_____
_____
_____
_____

Climate

_____
_____
_____
_____
_____

Name: _____

Biome Research 2

Plant Life

_____
_____
_____
_____
_____
_____
_____
_____
_____
_____
_____
_____
_____
_____
_____
_____
_____
_____
_____

Name: _____

Biome Research 3

Animal Life

_____
_____
_____
_____
_____
_____
_____
_____
_____
_____
_____
_____
_____
_____
_____
_____
_____
_____
_____
_____
_____
_____

Name: _____

The Earth's Biomes

Name That Biome

Put an **X** in the box of the biome where each plant or animal can be found. Some will be found in more than one biome. You may have to do some research.

	Desert	Forest	Ocean	Polar Region	Savanna	Prairies	Rainforest	Mountain	Fresh Water	Tundra		Desert	Forest	Ocean	Polar Region	Savanna	Prairies	Rainforest	Mountain	Fresh Water	Tundra
giraffe											parrot										
moose											saguaro										
killer whale											caribou										
antelope											frog										
polar bear											elephant										
elephant											raccoon										
parrot											deer										
camel											rabbit										
penguin											lichens/moss										
jaguar											sloth										
duckweed											toucan										
seal											kapok tree										
cougar											python										
duck											date palm										
bison											monkey										
mouse											musk ox										
lion											pika										
beaver											gorilla										
elk											walrus										
ostrich											acacia tree										
owl											hyena										
scorpion											eagle										

Skill: Classifying plants and animals in specific habitats.

69

Habitats

The Earth's Biomes

Drawing Landscapes

Note: These can be enlarged and pasted to each drawing.

This is the American desert. The sands of the desert are layered in many shades of orange, yellow, and brown. In the foreground, to the left, is a large saguaro cactus. A woodpecker is looking for insects on the cactus. Many different kinds of cacti can be seen growing on the desert floor. Several of the cacti plants have brightly-colored flowers. A hummingbird is gathering nectar from a large yellow cactus flower. In the foreground, a roadrunner is chasing a rattlesnake. A lizard is hiding in the shade of a large rock in the bottom right hand corner of the picture. A vulture is circling high in the sky, looking for food. Beneath the ground a kangaroo rat is hiding in its burrow. A scorpion is waiting for the rat to come out.

This is an Arctic landscape. Large pieces of ice are floating in the icy blue ocean. To the right, a herd of walruses are sitting on an island of ice. At the bottom and to the left is a family of polar bears. The male polar bear has just brought a seal to share for dinner. An arctic fox is looking and waiting for something to eat.

This is a picture of the South American rainforest found near the equator. There are many plants of all kinds growing everywhere. Vines are wrapped around trees and there are many colorful exotic flowers. Brightly-colored butterflies fly among the flowers. A jaguar sits on the branch of a tree, waiting for prey. At the top of the page is a thick canopy of leaves. A parrot and a toucan can be seen among the branches. A monkey can be seen swinging from a branch.

This is a picture of the African savanna. There are a few acacia trees growing far off, along the horizon. To the left is a large acacia tree. A weaver bird has built a nest in one of the branches. A python is wound around a branch of the tree. A giraffe is feeding on the leaves of the tree. In the foreground a lion, a lioness and two cubs lie among the tall grasses. Off in the distance an elephant is traveling west (north is top of the page.) Behind the lions, but not as far away as the elephant, is an antelope taking a drink at a water hole.

Habitats
Adaptations
Overview

This component introduces students to the concept of adaptations. They will investigate the various structural adaptations which allow animals and plants to survive in their habitats. They will be asked to observe the structural adaptations that allow fish to survive in water. The investigation 'Something's Fishy' can be completed without live specimens, however, it is recommended that the teacher purchase enough goldfish to provide each group of four with one live fish. If purchasing goldfish it is best to buy 'feeder' fish. They are very inexpensive (approx. $.10 - $0.25 each.) If using live fish for the investigation, simply cover over the black and white fish on the activity sheet and have the students use the space to draw the fish they are observing.

Learning Expectations

Students will:

1. Describe the structural adaptations of plants and animals that demonstrate a response of living things to their environment.
2. Recognize that animals and plants live in specific habitats because they are dependent on those habitats and have adapted to them.
3. Formulate questions about and identify the needs of animals and plants in a particular habitat, and explore possible answers to these questions and ways of meeting these needs.
4. Use appropriate vocabulary and scientific terminology when describing investigations, explorations and observations.
5. Communicate the procedures and results of investigations.

Planning Ahead

1. Duplicate the student activity pages and make booklets.
2. Collect magnifying glasses and magnifying boxes, microscopes and prepared slides.
3. Purchase goldfish for 'Something's Fishy' investigation if live specimens are used.
4. Locate films, filmstrips and videos about plant and animal adaptations (camouflage, etc.)
5. Locate books about animal adaptations, e.g. camouflage (see resource list.)
6. Find different types of plants for examination by the students, e.g. pine needles, cacti, maple keys, burdock seeds, etc. - anything that students can examine to determine how the plant has adapted to its environment.
7. Post pictures of animals and plants that clearly show adaptations , that is, pictures of cacti, giraffe, zebra, polar bear, ducks, birds, fish.
8. Check Science department for plant and animal specimens for examination by the students.

Habitats

Implementation Suggestions

1. Use a picture book or information card as a springboard to generate discussion of the term adaptation.

2. Ask students to list all the ways they are and are not adapted to survival in their environment. Make a chart. What do plants and animals do when the weather gets cold?

3. As an art activity, have students bring in a magazine picture of an animal that uses camouflage to survive in its habitat. The picture should be cut out and pasted onto a sheet of paper. Students should then draw a habitat for the animal which will camouflage the animal. The pictures can be displayed on a bulletin board.

4. Extend the activity on page 83 into an art activity by having students recreate their animal as a painting or sculpture, etc.

Resources

Book(s) recommended for introducing component.

Cole, Joanna, The Magic School Bus Gets All Dried Up - A Book About Deserts, Scholastic Canada Ltd., ©1996

Other useful books for implementing this topic:

Lauber, Patricia, Fur, Feathers and Flippers, Scholastic Canada Ltd., ©1994
National Geographic Society, Secrets of Animal Survival, National Geographic Society, ©1983

Habitats

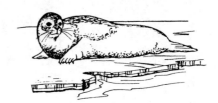

Adaptations

We find plants and animals living all over the world in many different types of environments. Humans would find it very difficult to live in some of the places where plants and animals are able to survive.

For an animal or plant to survive, it must be suited to its environment. Plants and animals survive in the biomes in which they live because they have certain features or adaptations. The shape and size of an animal's body must be suited to its surroundings. Large warm-blooded animals lose heat through their bodies more slowly than smaller animals. Thus, animals living in cold areas are often larger than their relatives in hot regions. Animals living in colder regions most often have thicker fur than animals in warmer biomes.

A polar bear would not be found living in a rainforest as it is not suited to life there. The thick layer of fat, called blubber, under the polar bear's skin keeps the bear warm in the icy ocean water of the polar regions. The polar bear can easily shake the water out of its long fur to keep its coat from freezing. It gets food from animals living in the same environment who have also adapted to life in the polar regions.

The way an animal moves is another adaptation. The cheetah lives in the savanna of East Africa. It has long legs and is the fastest of all land animals. It has excellent eye-sight and its spotted, tan colored coat blends in with the savanna grass to camouflage it from its prey. On the African savanna, animals must be able to move quickly to escape from their enemies on the open plains. There are few places where they can hide.

Many animals living in tropical rainforests must be able to hide from their enemies and their prey. Many animals of the rainforest use camouflage to blend in with the colors and shadows of the rainforest. Rainforest animals must also be able to move very quickly through the treetops. The monkey, for example, is very agile and can move through the trees like an acrobat.

Among the many animals living in the desert, is the camel. The camel is well adapted to life in this hot, dry biome with the heat, sand, wind and a lack of water. It would not survive in some other biomes, like the polar regions or the rainforest. The camel's body is adapted in several ways to life in the desert. In blowing sand it can close its nostrils into narrow slits, and its long eyelashes protect its eyes. Thick hair grows in a camel's ears which helps to keep out sand. The camel has wide foot pads that help it to walk on loose moving sand without sinking in.

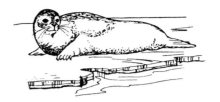

Habitats

Adaptations

In extremely hot and cold biomes, certain animals cannot stand their environments all year. They escape the heat or cold by going to sleep for long periods of time. In the desert, some animals sleep during the hottest months until the rains come. This sleep during the summer is called **aestivation**. In colder regions animals sleep in winter, when there is little food to be found. This sleep is called **hibernation**, and it allows the animal to conserve energy.

Birds are able to escape their harsh environments by flying to a more suitable climate during cold winter months. This escape is called **migration**.

Plants cannot move to escape the environment, so they must be perfectly suited to their environment. Like animals, plants need water to survive. All plants lose some water through their leaves, so when water is scarce plants must find ways to keep from losing it. Cactus plants have shallow, wide-spreading roots. They are able to soak up large amounts of water and store it for long periods of time in their thick, fleshy trunks and branches. They haven't any leaves but have a thick, waxy coating that helps keep the water inside. Coniferous trees have needle-like leaves with a waxy coating which prevent the trees from losing water. Deciduous trees drop their leaves in autumn to keep from losing water.

We can see that the shape and size of a plant or an animal's body helps it to survive in its environment. These characteristics are called adaptations. If the environment of a plant or animal slowly changes, then the plant or animal must change or adapt itself to the new environment or die out. If the environment changes too quickly, the plant or the animal will sometimes die.

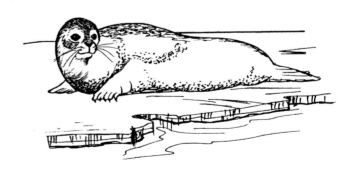

Name: _____

Adaptations

Activity 1

Write these words in your vocabulary chart:

feature	**blubber**	**aestivation**	**agile**
adaptation	**camouflage**	**hibernation**	
mammal	**conserve**	**migration**	

1. Match the correct word with its meaning:

   _____ adaptation   a) movement from one location to another

   _____ hibernation   b) a feature which allows a living thing to survive its
                              environment

   _____ migration   c) the sleep of an animal to escape the cold

   _____ aestivation   d) the sleep of an animal during summer to escape
                              the heat

2. Why are Arctic mammals usually large in size?

   _____

   _____

   _____

3. How is a monkey adapted to life in the rainforest?

   _____

   _____

4. Name three animals that use camouflage as a means of survival.

   _____, _____, _____

Name: _____

Adaptations

Activity 2

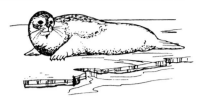

1. Explain how movement is an important adaptation of some animals. Give examples.

   _____
   _____
   _____
   _____
   _____
   _____
   _____
   _____
   _____

2. How is a camel adapted to life in the desert?

   _____
   _____
   _____
   _____
   _____
   _____
   _____
   _____
   _____
   _____
   _____

3. Explain how each of the following has adapted to its environment.

   a) cactus _____
   _____
   _____

   b) maple tree _____
   _____
   _____

Name: _____

Adaptations

A Perfect Match

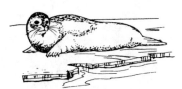

Complete the boxes by identifying the biome and continent in which each animal can be found, and give two ways the animal has adapted to its environment.

Animal	Biome	Adaptations
eagle		
polar bear		
giraffe		
mountain goat		
orangutan		
owl		
beaver		
jaguar		
caribou		

Skill: Describing the structural adaptations of plants and animals that demonstrate a response of living things to their environments.

Name: _____

Adaptations

Something's Fishy

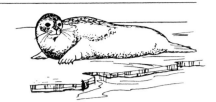

Fish are well adapted to life in water. Study the fish carefully. Tell how the different parts of the fish help it to survive in water.

1. _____
   _____
   _____

2. _____
   _____
   _____

3. _____
   _____
   _____

4. _____
   _____
   _____

5. _____
   _____
   _____

Skill: Describing the structural adaptations of plants and animals that demonstrate a response of living things to their environment.

Name: _____

Adaptations

Adapt an Animal

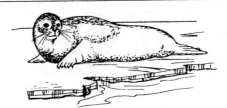

Create your own animal. Give it a name.
Label the parts of the animal which help it to survive in its environment.

_____

Describe your animal's habitat and how your animal is suited to its environment.

_____

_____

_____

_____

_____

_____

_____

_____

_____

Skill: Describing the structural adaptations of plants and animals that demonstrate a response of living things to their environment.

Habitats

Habitat Helpers

Overview

In this component students investigate the ways in which humans can positively and negatively affect the habitats of plants and animals. They will examine the dependence of humans on plants and animals. The component involves concepts related to endangered and extinct species, convservation and pollution.

Learning Expectations

Students will:

1. Recognize that animals and plants live in specific habitats because they are dependent on those habitats and have adapted to them.

2. Plan investigations and identify variables that need to be held constant to ensure fair and accurate testing.

3. Use appropriate vocabulary and scientific terminology when describing investigations, explorations and observations.

4. Communicate the procedures and results of investigations.

5. Describe ways in which humans are dependent on plants and animals.

6. Describe ways in which humans can affect the natural world.

7. Show the effects on plants and animals of the loss of their natural habitats.

8. Investigate ways in which the extinction of a plant or animal species affects the rest of the natural community and humans.

Planning Ahead

1. Duplicate the student activity pages and make booklets.

2. Locate films, filmstrips, etc. about pollution, conservation, endangered species, etc.

3. Ask your librarian for assistance in obtaining as many books about endangered species, adaptations, etc. as possible, as students will need to do some research.

4. Try to find some time in Language Arts or Social Science, etc. to teach and/or review research skills.

5. Ask your librarian for a class visit to the library and a lesson or two on using the library.

Habitats

Implementation Suggestions

1. Use one of the recommended picture books, the information card or a film about endangered animals, pollution, conservation, etc. to introduce the topic. There are many excellent films available in libraries.

2. Focus on research skills and explain to students that they will be researching an endangered animal.

3. Have students work in groups to brainstorm, research and make an oral presentation about:

   a) the uses of plants   d) the greenhouse effect

   b) air pollution   e) water pollution

   c) acid rain

Resources

Book(s) recommended for introducing the component:

Godkin, Celia, Ladybug Garden, Fitzhenry Whiteside, Toronto, ©1995
Hamilton, Virginia, Jaguarundi, Scholastic Canada Ltd., ©1995

Other useful books for implementing this topic:

Bailey, Jill, Save the Tiger, Raintree, Steck Vaughn, © (this is one of a series of books by Bailey)
Brooks, Felicity, Protecting Endangered Species, Usborn Publishing Ltd., ©1990
Cohen, Daniel, The Modern Ark: Saving Endangered Species, G.P. Putnam's Sons, ©1995
Facklam, Marjorie, And Then There Was One, Little, Brown and Company, Boston, ©1990
Harris, Colin, Protecting the Planet, Wayland Publishers Ltd., London, ©1992
Hickman, Pamela, The Kids Canadian Tree Book, Kids Can Press Ltd., Toronto, ©1995
Mullins, Patricia, V for Vanishing: An Alphabet of Endangered Animals, Harper Collins Children's Books, ©1994
Scimmemel, Schim, Dear Children of the Earth, Norwood Press, Inc., ©1994
Snow, Theodore P., A New True Book, Global Change, Children's Press Inc., Chicago, ©1990
The Earth Works Group, 50 Simple Things Kids Can Do to Save the Earth, Scholastic Canada Ltd., ©1990
Walker, Colin, Forests Forever, Lands End Publishing Ltd., New Zealand, ©1992

Habitats

Habitat Helpers

Today people are very concerned about the environment. Humans have done things to the earth which have had a very negative effect on the environment. People are rapidly changing the earth with the things they do. When you hear scientists talk about global change, they are referring to changes to the earth that are caused by people. Most of these changes have taken place in the last hundred years. Some of these changes are bad for the plants, animals and people living on the earth.

Every time humans make changes or interfere with the environment, animal and plant habitats are destroyed and lost forever. When large ecosystems like forests are cut down, many species of plants are destroyed. Plants and animals not only provide us with food but are used for medicine, clothing, building, oil and many other products we use every day. Without plants to hold the soil in place, flooding occurs and valuable soil is washed away.

Humans have always depended on plants and animals for food. Some animals have been hunted for sport or for a particular part of their bodies such as skin, fur, tusks or horns. Other plants and animals have been looked upon as pests and have been poisoned or sprayed with **insecticides** and **pesticides**. Sometimes **chemicals** and poisons meant to kill one particular species have killed many other plants and animals.

Humans have destroyed the habitats of animals by cutting trees for lumber. They have drained swamps and cleared forests to make room for farms, homes and factories. All over the world seas, lakes and rivers have been **polluted** by humans, and millions of water creatures have been killed. Water is polluted mainly by factory waste and waste from homes and oil spills. Other chemicals, like pesticides and insecticides that have been sprayed on land wash into the rivers, lakes and streams killing plants and animals. Many times chemicals are found in plants which are eaten by animals and humans.

Our earth is mostly water, and every living thing depends on water for life. Humans are not keeping the waters of the earth very clean. We pollute the oceans, lakes, rivers and streams with poisonous waste from factories, insecticides, pesticides, **fertilizers** and oil spills. We dump garbage from ships into the oceans.

Acid rain is caused when gases mix with the water in the air and make it acidic. The gases are released into the air from factories and cars. Acid rain is very harmful to plants, forests, rivers and lakes, and to the animals which live in them.

Habitats

Habitat Helpers

The air we breathe is also polluted by the smoke from factories, homes and cars. Harmful gases are put into the air. This pollution makes it hard for people, animals, plants and trees to stay healthy. In the cities we find **smog** which we can see hanging in the sky, making it difficult for people and animals to breathe.

Many plants and animals on our earth have disappeared or are endangered, in danger of disappearing forever. When a living thing dies out and can't be found on the earth again, it is said to be **extinct** or gone forever. It will never be on the earth again. Today hundreds of birds and animals are **endangered**. It is natural for living things to die out over time, however the interference of humans with the natural environment is endangering or causing plants and animals to become extinct at a very fast rate.

Around the world, there are many organizations working to protect the habitats of plants and animals. Together all the organizations are called the 'Green Movement.' Whenever a habitat is in danger the 'Green' organizations try to help. The most important job of these organizations is educating people about how important it is that we help to save the habitats of plants and animals.

As a junior ecologist you can do many things to help the earth. You now understand the important role of every living thing on the earth. You understand that every plant and animal has a role to play in the balance of nature. You understand that even the tiniest plant or animal is important to an ecosystem. You understand how important it is to preserve habitats. If everyone decides to care and tries hard to protect his/her environment, perhaps we can stop any further harm to the earth.

Name: _____

Habitat and Humans

Activity 1

Write these words in your vocabulary chart:

endangered	pesticide	pest	global
extinct	insecticide	interfere	fertilizer
pollute	chemicals	exterminated	

1. Write the definitions of the following words:

   a) extinct _____

   _____

   b) endangered _____

   _____

   c) pesticide _____

   _____

   d) insecticide _____

   _____

   e) exterminated _____

   _____

   f) pollute _____

   _____

2. Explain how chemicals like insecticides that are sprayed on plants affect animals and humans.

   _____

   _____

   _____

   _____

   _____

   _____

Habitat and Humans

Activity 2

1. Think of three plants or animals that humans try to get rid of. Explain why these plants or animals are considered pests.

   a) _____ - _____
   _____
   _____

   b) _____ - _____
   _____
   _____

   c) _____ - _____
   _____
   _____

2. Choose one of the plants or animals from question one and do some research. Find out about its ecological niche. Research and then discuss your findings with your classmates. Have your feelings about the plant or animal changed? Explain.

   _____
   _____
   _____
   _____
   _____
   _____
   _____
   _____
   _____
   _____
   _____
   _____
   _____

Name: _____

Habitat and Humans

Activity 3

Plants and animals are very useful to humans for purposes other than food. Do some research and list as many uses as you can for plants and animals (other than food.) Try to identify which part of the plant or animal is used and what it is used for. Write your information in the charts below.

Name of plant	Part of the plant used	What it is used for

Name of animal	Part of the animal used	What it is used for

Habitat and Humans

Helping Habitats

Choose an area near your home that now provides or once provided habitats for plants and animals. Thinking about what you have learned about habitats, make a plan for improving the area to attract more plants and animals.

Describe the area you are trying to improve.

_____
_____
_____

Why do you think this is an area that needs help?

_____
_____
_____

Was this area ever a home for plants and animals? What happened?

_____
_____
_____

List five things you would do to make the area more suitable for plants and animals.

1. _____
   _____

2. _____
   _____

3. _____
   _____

4. _____
   _____

5. _____
   _____

Name: _____

Endangered Species Report 1

_____

Appearance

Habitat

_____
_____
_____

Name: _____

Endangered Species Report 2

Food:

_____

_____

_____

_____

Enemies:

_____

_____

_____

_____

_____

Interesting Facts:

_____

_____

_____

_____

_____

Why Endangered?:

_____

_____

_____

_____

What is being done to help?:

_____

_____

_____

_____

_____

Bibliography:

1. _____

2. _____

Habitats and Humans

Let's Be Ecologists!

You've thought very carefully about your interesting and very important job as a junior ecologist. You know just what to say to convince a group of students that they should be interested in the preservation of plant and animal habitats. You've decided to write a speech to convince them that they can help. Write your speech below.

_____

_____

_____

_____

_____

_____

_____

_____

_____

_____

_____

_____

_____

_____

_____

_____

_____

_____

_____

_____

_____

_____

_____

_____

_____

_____

Name: _____

Habitats Helpers
Ecology Game
Project

Your task is to plan and create a game about 'Habitats.' It can be a board game, card game or any other type of game that can be played at a table.

Your game should
_____   include your plans
_____   be suitable for age 8 to adult
_____   be packaged in a neat and interesting way
_____   have an interesting name
_____   include rules and instructions

Include as many of the following concepts as possible: producers, consumers, herbivores, carnivores, omnivores, adaptations, extinct, endangered, pollution, insecticides, and pesticiedes.

Your game should be completed by _____.

- -

Game Plan

Name of game: _____

Type of game (card, board, etc.): _____

Age suitable for: _____

Number of players : _____

How the game is played: _____
_____
_____
_____
_____
_____
_____
_____

Diagram

Habitats

Crossword Puzzle

ACROSS

1. a species that needs protection
5. an area of wet land
7. this biome is disappearing
9. very hot area with much sand
11. a good home for a bat
13. a bear likes to call this home for the winter
16. the `Great Grey' is one
18. this makes up three-fifths of the earth's surface
19. what plants give off

DOWN

1. many communities of living things
2. trout can be found living here
3. cattails call this home
4. in some areas this is called savanna
6. home to the frog
8. home of the elk
10. made up of minerals
12. large predator bird
14. type of goose
15. seed from a coniferous tree
17. a good habitat when rotting

Habitats

Crossword Puzzle

Habitats

Wordsearch

```
F O N H B B A L A N C E N K O G T R G
H U M I D J E C O S Y S T E M J G K R
H J D E C I D U O U S Y R T H E O E A
Y T E N H J N I O M U D A P A M P A S
Y I L I C H E N O E M I S A B R E P S
P O I C V F E H J Y R U E W I T Y U L
N M T H C G R E S A E Y N J T I T E A
E P O E Y H P F H G T O T I A T T F N
L R O X J B O T A N I S T H T H F T D
J I O Y R D L Y U T H H P R E Y B U A
B H T V N H A C A C T U S B H T R N G
O C O L I O R L G F Y O B T R R N D S
E L B I T N U T R I E N T E R A B R P
M I B I G P M F T R E R G T V A G A E
K M I S O I L O J W E T L A N D S H C
S A N P L M I U Y S R F S R F A R F I
O T I J K V E G E T A T I O N P I U E
M E N E R G Y D A R F O R E S T O G S
```

vegetation	polar	community	soil	wetlands
climate	pampas	biome	prey	savanna
habitat	ecosystem	nutrient	niche	forest
energy	oxygen	cactus	species	humid
omnivore	lichen	botanist	balance	
grassland	tundra	adapt	deciduous	

OTM-2104 • SSB1-104 Habitats

Name: _____

Habitats

Quiz 1

ecosystem	ecology	habitat	energy
producer	carnivore	chlorophyll	consumer
light	ecologist	sun	omnivore

1. Choose a word from the box above to complete each sentence. Be careful because there are more words than you will need.

    a) An animal that eats other animals is called a _____.

    b) The green substance found in plants is called _____.

    c) The study of why living things live where they do is called _____.

    d) Another word for 'home' is _____.

    e) A large community of habitats is called an _____.

    f) All food chains begin with the _____.

    g) A form of energy necessary for most plants to grow is _____.

    h) A plant is a _____, since it traps the sun's energy and uses it first.

    i) A human being is an _____.

    j) All living things in a food chain receive _____ from the sun.

2. Write **T** if the sentence is **True** or **F** if the sentence is **False**.

    ☐ a) A wolf is a producer.

    ☐ b) Man is at the top of any food chain.

    ☐ c) Photosynthesis means "making food with soil."

    ☐ d) Bears are omnivores.

    ☐ e) Farmers like to get rid of owls in their barns.

Habitats

Quiz 2

1. One spring, Farmer Green had a very good field of wheat. Whenever he saw any birds in his field, he got his gun and shot as many of the birds as he could. In the middle of the summer he found that his wheat was being ruined by insects. Explain what was happening.

   _____
   _____
   _____
   _____

2. Choose an animal or plant from any part of the world. Describe its habitat and how it is adapted to survival there.

   _____
   _____
   _____
   _____
   _____

3. List three ways a camel is adapted to life in the desert.

   a) _____
   b) _____
   c) _____

4. Name three problems with the earth's environment that has been caused by humans.

   a) _____
   b) _____
   c) _____

5. What is the ecological niche of an owl?

   _____
   _____
   _____

Habitats
Quiz 3

1. Name the four things every living thing needs in order to survive.

   a) _____   b) _____

   c) _____   d) _____

2. Write a definition for each of the following:

   a) hibernation _____
   _____

   b) decomposer _____
   _____

   c) carnivore _____
   _____

   d) population _____
   _____

   e) vegetation _____
   _____

3. Name three grassland areas of the world and a continent on which they can be found.

Name of grassland	A continent where found

4. Using phrases, describe the tundra region of Canada.

   _____ ,   _____ ,

   _____ ,   _____ .

What is Ecology?
Activity 1: *(page 21)*
1. one who studies plants and animals as they are found in nature
2. botanist

Activity 2: *(page 22)*
1. To examine carefully in a search of facts, knowledge or information.
2. Dessert is much tastier as it is the last part of a lunch or dinner, and a desert is a dry region usually covered with sand.
3. All the plants and animals sharing a habitat.
4. Answer will vary.
5. Answers will vary.

What Would You Like To Be? *(page 23)*
A to O - drop the 'y' and add 'ist'
1. f **2.** g **3.** h **4.** d **5.** o **6.** c **7.** b **8.** a **9.** e **10.** m **11.** k **12.** n
13. l **14.** j **15.** i

E is for Ecology: *(page 24)*
1. environment **2.** earth **3.** ecologist **4.** evaporation **5.** endangered **6.** energy
7. extinct **8.** erosion **9.** ecosystem **10.** evergreen

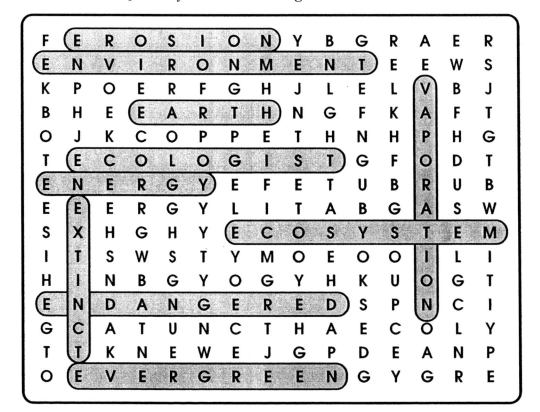

A Habitat is a Home:
Activity 1: *(page 28)*

1.

c	environment	a	to try to win something
h	survive	b	the lose top layer of the earth's surface
g	shelter	c	the surroundings in which a plant or animal lives
d	habitat	d	the place where a plant or animal usually lives
f	climate	e	the plants and animals that live in balance with each other and the soils and climate around them
b	soil	f	the usual weather a place has all year
e	ecosystem	g	something that protects or covers
a	compete	h	to stay alive

2. **a)** food **b)** water **c)** space **d)** shelter
3. Answers will vary.

Hunting for a Home: *(page 34)*
Answers will vary depending on the area and research books used by the students.

Food Chains:
Activity 1: *(page 38)*
1. **a)** F **b)** T **c)** F **d)** F **e)** F **f)** T **g)** F **h)** T **i)** T **j)** F
2. **a)** animal that feeds on other animals; meat-eater
   b) animal that eats both plants and other animals
   c) animal that eats plants only

Activity 2: *(page 39)*
1.

Herbivore	Carnivore	Omnivore	Insectivore
deer	owl	bear	anteater
worm	hawk	human	frog
rabbit	seal	baboon	
moose		skunk	
grasshopper		robin	

2. an animal that actively hunts other animals for food
3. animals hunted by predators for food

Activity 3: *(page 40)*

1. sun, light, heat, energy, producers, roots, stems, leaves, fruit, seeds, food, consumers, food chains

Making Food Chains: *(page 41)*

Answers will vary.

How Do plants Make Food: *(page 43)*

1. Energy from the sun in the form of heat and light is trapped and made into food.
2. Carbon dioxide from the air is taken into the plant.
3. Water and nutrients from the soil are taken into the land through roots in the soil.
4. Oxygen is given off into the air.

Wolf Island: *(page 47)*

1. mice, deer, rabbits, squirrels, foxes, and many different kinds of birds
3. The island ecosystem deteriorates because the food chain is missing a link. The island becomes overrun by animals, vegetation disappears, and animals starve.

Each to Its Niche:

Activity 1: *(page 52)*

1. the job an animal does and its way of life
2. **a)** eats young shoots of trees and bark, lives in deciduous forest, hunted by large predators
   b) eats rotting plant material, movement through the soil breaks it up
   c) breathe through gills, live in moist places, decompose plant material for bacteria to act upon
   d) eats seeds and nuts, buries seeds and nuts, hibernates during winter
   e) eats mostly earthworms, makes nest in trees, sometimes migrates to warmer weather
   f) large predator bird, eats mice and other small rodents
   g) predator, eats deer and small animals, hunts and lives in packs

Activity 2: *(page 53)*

Answers will vary.

The Earth's Biomes:

Activity 1: *(page 62)*

1. A large natural region where certain kinds of plants grow and animals that use the plants for food can be found living.
2. **a)** temperature   **b)** rainfall   **c)** wind   **d)** amount of light
3. plant life
4. coniferous
5. broad leaves
6. 200 cm (70 inches)
7. rain, snow
8. prairies, plains, savanna, pampas, steppes

Activity 2: *(page 63)*

1.

Tropical Grassland	tough grasses, few trees
Desert	cacti or palms
Coniferous Forest	evergreens
Tundra	mosses and lichens
Polar Region	treeless
Rainforest	thick plant growth
Deciduous Forest	maples, oaks, poplars

2. oceans, freshwater lakes, rivers and streams, wetlands

3.

Coniferous Trees	Deciduous Trees
pine	maple
spruce	poplar
cedar	oak
fir, etc.	birch, etc.

Mapping Activity: *(page 65)*

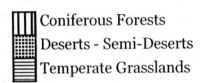 Polar Regions   Tropical Grasslands   Coniferous Forests
Tundra   Mountains   Deserts - Semi-Deserts
Deciduous Forests   Tropical Forests   Temperate Grasslands

2. Tropical Grasslands (savanna,) Deserts and Semi-Deserts
3. Answer will Vary (Canada - coniferous Forest)
4. Oceans
5. Tropical Grasslands (savanna,) Deserts and Semi-Deserts
6. Northern
7. Equator
8. Tropical Forest
9. North America and Asia

Adaptations:

Activity 1: *(page 75)*

1. b); c); a); d)
2. Large warm-blood mammals lose heat through their bodies more slowly than smaller animals.
3. Very agile. They can move through the trees more quickly.
4. giraffe, zebra, lion

Activity 2: *(page 76)*

1. movement important in areas where animals cannot hide and must escape quickly, catch prey e.g. monkey, cheetah, gazelle
2. can go for long periods without water, long eyelashes, can close nostrils, thick hair in ears, wide pads on feet
3. a) shallow, wide-spreading roots, can store large amounts of water, thin waxy needles that don't lose water, thick fleshy trunks
   b) maple trees have deep roots and lose leaves in winter to prevent water loss

A Perfect Match: *(page 77)*

eagle - mountain - large sharp claws, keen eyesight, strong sharp beak
polar bear - polar region - thick fur
giraffe - savanna - long neck, spots for camouflage
mountain goat - mountains
orangutan - rainforest - strong, agile
owl - forest - keen eyesight, large claws, powerful wings for moving quietly
beaver - ponds - large sharp teeth, strong flat tail
jaguar - rainforest - fast, sharp teeth and claws
caribou - large, thick fur to withstand cold, herbivorous, feeds on moss and lichens, hooves

Something's Fishy: *(page 78)*

1. gills - for taking oxygen from the water
2. scales - for quick movement through the water, no resistance
3. fins - for movement and steering
4. tail - strong, for steering and speed
5. streamlined body - for easy movement through the water

Habitat Helpers:

Activity 1: *(page 84)*

1. a) no longer on the earth, gone forever
   b) in danger of disappearing forever if steps are not taken to protect its habitat
   c) chemicals used to get rid of unwanted animals
   d) a poison or other substance used to get rid of unwanted insects
   e) destroyed, killed, wiped out
   f) to make harmful for living things

2. Chemicals and pesticides harm the animals and humans that eat the plants. The chemicals are often washed into water sources, harming water animals and polluting water supplies.

Activity 2: *(page 85)*

1. Answers will vary.
2. Answers will vary - Hopefully, through research, students will discover that every living thing has a job and its eradication can upset the balance of nature, e.g. the wolf.

Crossword Puzzle: *(page 93)*

Across/Down filled answers:

- 1. ENDANGERED
- ECOSYSTEM (down)
- 2. STEAM / STREAM
- 3. MARSH
- 4. GRASSLAND
- 5. SWAMP
- 6. PRON... (PON?)
- 7. RAINFOREST
- 8. TUNDRA
- 9. DESERT
- 10. ROOK / ROT
- 11. CAVE
- 12. EAGLE
- 13. DEN / DEND
- 14. CANADA
- 15. C
- 16. OWL
- 17. LOG
- 18. OCEANE / OCEAN
- 19. OXYGEN

Wordsearch: *(page 94)*

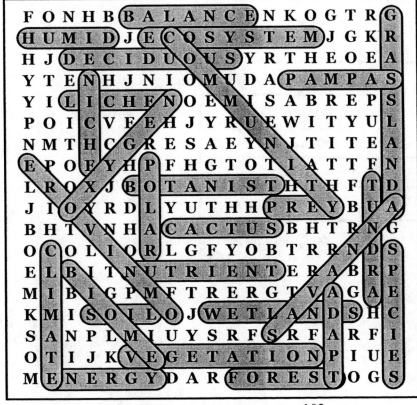

```
F O N H B B A L A N C E N K O G T R G
H U M I D J E C O S Y S T E M J G K R
H J D E C I D U O U S Y R T H E O E A
Y T E N H J N I O M U D A P A M P A S
Y I L I C H E N O E M I S A B R E P S
P O I C V E E H J Y R U E W I T Y U L
N M T H C G R E S A E Y N J T I T E A
E P O E Y H P F H G T O T I A T T F N
L R O X J B O T A N I S T H T H F T D
J I O Y R D L Y U T H H P R E Y B U A
B H T V N H A C A C T U S B H T R N G
O C O L I O R L G F Y O B T R R N D S
E L B I T N U T R I E N T E R A B R P
M I B I G P M F T R E R G T V A G A E
K M I S O I L O J W E T L A N D S H C
S A N P L M I U Y S R F S R F A R F I
O T I J K V E G E T A T I O N P I U E
M E N E R G Y D A R F O R E S T O G S
```

Quiz 1: *(page 95)*

1. **a)** carnivore **b)** chlorophyll **c)** ecology **d)** habitat **e)** ecosystem **f)** sun
   g) light **h)** producer **i)** omnivore **j)** energy
2. **a)** F **b)** T **c)** F (making food with light) **d)** T
   e) F (they eat the mice which eat the grain)

Quiz 2: *(page 96)*

1. Once the birds, which ate the insects, were eliminated, the insects were free to eat the crops.
2. Answer will vary.
3. **a)** camel is adapted with wide flat feet for walking easily on sand
   b) long eyelashes for keeping sand out of their eyes
   c) hair in ears to keep out sand
   d) nostrils which close to keep out sand
   e) they can survive for long periods without water
4. **a)** acid rain
   b) air pollution
   c) water pollution
   d) greenhouse effect
   e) damage to ozone layer
   f) extinction and endangeerment of plants and animals
5. Nocturnal hunter, eater of mice and other small animals.

Quiz 3: *(page 97)*

1. **a)** food **b)** shelter **c)** water **d)** space
2. **a)** the winter sleep of animals to escape cold and hunger
   b) a living thing which helps to break down dead rotting plant and animal material
   c) eats only meat
   d) the total number of one species in an area
   e) plant life
3.

Name of grassland	A continent where found
prairies, plains	North America
savanna	Africa
pampas	South America
steppes	Eurasia

4. tundra (very large plain) (no trees) (mosses, lichens and small shrubs)
   (permafrost most of the year) (very cold and windy)

Publication Listing

See Dealer or
www.sslearning.com
For Pricing
1-800-463-6367

Code #	Title and Grade
SSC1-12	A Time of Plenty Gr. 2
SSN1-92	Abel's Island NS 4-6
SSF1-16	Aboriginal Peoples of Canada Gr. 7-8
SSK1-31	Addition & Subtraction Drills Gr. 1-3
SSK1-28	Addition Drills Gr. 1-3
SSY1-04	Addition Gr. 1-3
SSN1-174	Adv. of Huckle Berry Finn NS 7-8
SSB1-63	African Animals Gr 4-6
SSB1-29	All About Bears Gr. 1-2
SSF1-08	All About Boats Gr. 2-3
SSJ1-02	All About Canada Gr. 2
SSB1-54	All About Cattle Gr. 4-6
SSN1-10	All About Colours Gr. P-1
SSB1-93	All About Dinosaurs Gr. 2
SSN1-14	All About Dragons Gr. 3-5
SSB1-07	All About Elephants Gr. 3-4
SSB1-68	All About Fish Gr. 4-6
SSN1-39	All About Giants Gr. 2-3
SSH1-15	All About Jobs Gr. 1-3
SSH1-05	All About Me Gr. 1
SSA1-02	All About Mexico Gr. 4-6
SSR1-28	All About Nouns Gr. 5-7
SSF1-09	All About Planes Gr. 2-3
SSB1-33	All About Plants Gr. 2-3
SSR1-29	All About Pronouns Gr. 5-7
SSB1-12	All About Rabbits Gr. 2-3
SSB1-58	All About Spiders Gr. 4-6
SSA1-03	All About the Desert Gr. 4-6
SSA1-04	All About the Ocean Gr. 5-7
SSZ1-01	All About the Olympics Gr. 2-4
SSB1-49	All About the Sea Gr. 4-6
SSK1-06	All About Time Gr. 4-6
SSF1-07	All About Trains Gr. 2-3
SSH1-18	All About Transportation Gr. 2
SSB1-01	All About Trees Gr. 4-6
SSB1-61	All About Weather Gr. 7-8
SSB1-06	All About Whales Gr. 3-4
SSPC-26	All Kinds of Clocks B/W Pictures
SSB1-110	All Kinds of Structures Gr. 1
SSH1-19	All Kinds of Vehicles Gr. 3
SSF1-01	Amazing Aztecs Gr. 4-6
SSB1-92	Amazing Earthworms Gr. 2-3
SSJ1-50	Amazing Facts in Canadian History Gr. 4-6
SSB1-32	Amazing Insects Gr. 4-6
SSN1-132	Amelia Bedelia–Camping NS 1-3
SSN1-68	Amelia Bedelia NS 1-3
SSN1-155	Amelia Bedelia-Surprise Shower NS 1-3
SSA1-13	America The Beautiful Gr. 4-6
SSN1-57	Amish Adventure NS 7-8
SSF1-02	Ancient China Gr. 4-6
SSF1-18	Ancient Egypt Gr. 4-6
SSF1-21	Ancient Greece Gr. 4-6
SSF1-19	Ancient Rome Gr. 4-6
SSQ1-06	Animal Town – Big Book Pkg 1-3
SSQ1-02	Animals Prepare Winter – Big Book Pkg 1-3
SSN1-150	Animorphs the Invasion NS 4-6
SSN1-53	Anne of Green Gables NS 7-8
SSB1-40	Apple Celebration Gr. 4-6
SSB1-04	Apple Mania Gr. 2-3
SSB1-38	Apples are the Greatest Gr. P-K
SSB1-59	Arctic Animals Gr. 4-6
SSN1-162	Arnold Lobel Author Study Gr. 2-3
SSPC-22	Australia B/W Pictures
SSA1-05	Australia Gr. 5-8
SSM1-03	Autumn in the Woodlot Gr. 2-3
SSM1-08	Autumn Wonders Gr. 1
SSN1-41	Baby Sister for Frances NS 1-3
SSPC-19	Back to School B/W Pictures
SSC1-33	Back to School Gr. 2-3
SSN1-224	Banner in the Sky NS 7-8
SSN1-36	Bargain for Frances NS 1-3
SSB1-82	Bats Gr. 4-6
SSN1-71	BB – Drug Free Zone NS Gr. 1-3
SSN1-88	BB – In the Freaky House NS 1-3
SSN1-78	BB – Media Madness NS 1-3
SSN1-69	BB – Wheelchair Commando NS 1-3
SSN1-119	Be a Perfect Person-3 Days NS 4-6
SSC1-15	Be My Valentine Gr. 1
SSD1-01	Be Safe Not Sorry Gr. P-1
SSN1-09	Bear Tales Gr. 2-4
SSB1-28	Bears Gr. 4-6
SSN1-202	Bears in Literature Gr. 1-3
SSN1-40	Beatrix Potter Gr. 2-4
SSN1-129	Beatrix Potter: Activity Biography 2-4
SSB1-47	Beautiful Bugs Gr. 1
SSB1-21	Beavers Gr. 3-5
SSN1-257	Because of Winn-Dixie NS Gr. 4-6
SSN1-33	Bedtime for Frances NS 1-3
SSN1-114	Best Christmas Pageant Ever NS 4-6
SSN1-32	Best Friends for Frances NS 1-3
SSB1-39	Best Friends Pets Gr. P-K
SSN1-185	BFG NS Gr. 4-6
SSN1-35	Birthday for Frances NS Gr. 1-3
SSN1-107	Borrowers NS Gr. 4-6
SSC1-16	Bouquet of Valentines Gr. 2
SSN1-29	Bread & Jam for Frances NS 1-3
SSN1-63	Bridge to Terabithia NS Gr. 4-6
SSY1-24	BTS Numeración Gr. 1-3
SSY1-25	BTS Adición Gr. 1-3
SSY1-26	BTS Sustracción Gr. 1-3
SSY1-27	BTS Fonética Gr. 1-3
SSY1-28	BTS Leer para Entender Gr. 1-3
SSY1-29	BTS Uso de las Mayúsculas y Reglas de Puntuación Gr. 1-3
SSY1-30	BTS Composición de Oraciones Gr. 1-3
SSY1-31	BTS Composici13n de Historias Gr. 1-3
SSN1-256	Bud, Not Buddy NS Gr. 4-6
SSB1-31	Bugs, Bugs & More Bugs Gr. 2-3
SSR1-07	Building Word Families L.V. 1-2
SSR1-05	Building Word Families S.V. 1-2
SSN1-204	Bunnicula NS Gr. 4-6
SSB1-80	Butterflies & Caterpillars Gr. 1-2
SSN1-164	Call It Courage NS Gr. 7-8
SSN1-67	Call of the Wild NS Gr. 7-8
SSJ1-41	Canada & It's Trading Partners 6-8
SSPC-28	Canada B/W Pictures
SSN1-173	Canada Geese Quilt NS Gr. 4-6
SSJ1-01	Canada Gr. 1
SSJ1-33	Canada's Capital Cities Gr. 4-6
SSJ1-43	Canada's Confederation Gr. 7-8
SSF1-04	Canada's First Nations Gr. 7-8
SSJ1-51	Canada's Landmarks Gr. 1-3
SSJ1-48	Canada's Landmarks Gr. 4-6
SSJ1-42	Canada's Traditions & Celeb. Gr. 1-3
SSB1-45	Canadian Animals Gr. 1-2
SSJ1-37	Canadian Arctic Inuit Gr. 2-3
SSJ1-53	Canadian Black History Gr. 4-8
SSJ1-57	Canadian Comprehension Gr. 1-2
SSJ1-58	Canadian Comprehension Gr. 3-4
SSJ1-59	Canadian Comprehension Gr. 5-6
SSJ1-46	Canadian Industries Gr. 4-6
SSK1-12	Canadian Problem Solving Gr. 4-6
SSJ1-38	Canadian Provinces & Terr. Gr. 4-6
SSY1-07	Capitalization & Punctuation Gr. 1-3
SSN1-198	Captain Courageous NS Gr. 7-8
SSK1-11	Cars Problem Solving Gr. 3-4
SSN1-154	Castle in the Attic NS Gr. 4-6
SSF1-31	Castles & Kings Gr. 4-6
SSN1-144	Cat Ate My Gymsuit NS Gr. 4-6
SSPC-38	Cats B/W Pictures
SSB1-50	Cats – Domestic & Wild Gr. 4-6
SSN1-34	Cats in Literature Gr. 3-6
SSN1-212	Cay NS Gr. 7-8
SSM1-09	Celebrate Autumn Gr. 4-6
SSC1-39	Celebrate Christmas Gr. 4-6
SSC1-31	Celebrate Easter Gr. 4-6
SSC1-23	Celebrate Shamrock Day Gr. 2
SSM1-11	Celebrate Spring Gr. 4-6
SSC1-13	Celebrate Thanksgiving R. 3-4
SSM1-06	Celebrate Winter Gr. 4-6
SSB1-107	Cells, Tissues & Organs Gr. 7-8
SSB1-101	Characteristics of Flight Gr. 4-6
SSN1-66	Charlie & Chocolate Factory NS 4-6
SSN1-23	Charlotte's Web NS Gr. 4-6
SSB1-37	Chicks N'Ducks Gr. 2-4
SSA1-09	China Today Gr. 5-8
SSN1-70	Chocolate Fever NS Gr. 4-6
SSN1-241	Chocolate Touch NS Gr. 4-6
SSC1-38	Christmas Around the World Gr. 4-6
SSPC-42	Christmas B/W Pictures
SST1-08A	Christmas Gr. JK/SK
SST1-08B	Christmas Gr. 1
SST1-08C	Christmas Gr. 2-3
SSC1-04	Christmas Magic Gr. 1
SSC1-03	Christmas Tales Gr. 2-3
SSG1-06	Cinematography Gr. 5-8
SSPC-13	Circus B/W Pictures
SSF1-03	Circus Magic Gr. 3-4
SSJ1-52	Citizenship/Immigration Gr. 4-8
SSN1-104	Classical Poetry Gr. 7-12
SSN1-227	Color Gr. 1-3
SSN1-203	Colour Gr. 1-3
SSN1-135	Come Back Amelia Bedelia NS 1-3
SSH1-11	Community Helpers Gr. 1-3
SSK1-02	Concept Cards & Activities Gr. P-1
SSN1-183	Copper Sunrise NS Gr. 7-8
SSN1-86	Corduroy & Pocket Corduroy NS 1-3
SSN1-124	Could Dracula Live in Wood NS 4-6
SSN1-148	Cowboy's Don't Cry NS Gr. 7-8
SSR1-01	Creativity with Food Gr. 4-8
SSB1-34	Creatures of the Sea Gr. 2-4
SSN1-208	Curse of the Viking Grave NS 7-8
SSN1-134	Danny Champion of World NS 4-6
SSN1-98	Danny's Run NS Gr. 7-8
SSK1-21	Data Management Gr. 4-6
SSB1-53	Dealing with Dinosaurs Gr. 4-6
SSN1-178	Dear Mr. Henshaw NS Gr. 4-6
SSB1-22	Deer Gr. 3-5
SSPC-20	Desert B/W Pictures
SSJ1-40	Development of Western Canada Gr. 7-8
SSA1-16	Development of Manufacturing 7-9
SSN1-105	Dicken's Christmas NS Gr. 7-8
SSN1-62	Different Dragons NS Gr. 4-6
SSPC-21	Dinosaurs B/W Pictures
SSB1-16	Dinosaurs Gr. 1
SST1-02A	Dinosaurs Gr. JK/SK
SST1-02B	Dinosaurs Gr. 1
SST1-02C	Dinosaurs Gr. 2-3
SSN1-175	Dinosaurs in Literature Gr. 1-3
SSJ1-26	Discover Nova Scotia Gr. 5-7
SSJ1-36	Discover Nunavut Territory Gr. 5-7
SSJ1-25	Discover Ontario Gr. 5-7
SSJ1-24	Discover PEI Gr. 5-7
SSJ1-22	Discover Québec Gr. 5-7
SSL1-01	Discovering the Library Gr. 2-3
SSB1-106	Diversity of Living Things Gr. 4-6
SSK1-27	Division Drills Gr. 4-6
SSB1-30	Dogs – Wild & Tame Gr. 4-6
SSPC-31	Dogs B/W Pictures
SSN1-196	Dog's Don't Tell Jokes NS Gr. 4-6
SSN1-182	Door in the Wall NS Gr. 4-6
SSB1-87	Down by the Sea Gr. 1-3
SSN1-189	Dr. Jeckyll & Mr. Hyde NS Gr. 4-6
SSG1-07	Dragon Trivia Gr. P-8
SSN1-102	Dragon's Egg NS Gr. 4-6
SSN1-16	Dragons in Literature Gr. 3-6
SSC1-06	Early Christmas Gr. 3-5
SSB1-109	Earth's Crust Gr. 6-8
SSC1-21	Easter Adventures Gr. 3-4
SSC1-17	Easter Delights Gr. P-K
SSC1-19	Easter Surprises Gr. 1
SSPC-12	Egypt B/W Pictures
SSN1-255	Egypt Game NS Gr. 4-6
SSF1-28	Egyptians Today & Yesterday Gr. 2-3
SSJ1-49	Elections in Canada Gr. 4-8
SSB1-108	Electricity Gr. 4-6
SSN1-02	Elves & the Shoemaker NS Gr. 1-3
SSH1-14	Emotions Gr. P-2
SSB1-85	Energy Gr. 4-6
SSN1-108	English Language Gr. 10-12
SSN1-156	Enjoying Eric Wilson Series Gr. 5-7
SSB1-64	Environment Gr. 4-6
SSR1-12	ESL Teaching Ideas Gr. K-8
SSN1-258	Esperanza Rising NS Gr. 4-6
SSR1-22	Exercises in Grammar Gr. 6
SSR1-23	Exercises in Grammar Gr. 7
SSR1-24	Exercises in Grammar Gr. 8
SSF1-20	Exploration Gr. 4-6
SSF1-15	Explorers & Mapmakers of Canada 7-8
SSJ1-54	Exploring Canada Gr. 1-3
SSJ1-56	Exploring Canada Gr. 1-6
SSJ1-55	Exploring Canada Gr. 4-6
SSH1-20	Exploring My School and Community Gr. 1
SSPC-39	Fables B/W Pictures
SSN1-15	Fables Gr. 4-6
SSN1-04	Fairy Tale Magic Gr. 3-5
SSPC-11	Fairy Tales B/W Pictures
SSN1-11	Fairy Tales Gr. 1-2
SSN1-199	Family Under the Bridge NS 4-6
SSPC-41	Famous Canadians B/W Pictures
SSJ1-12	Famous Canadians Gr. 4-8
SSN1-210	Fantastic Mr. Fox NS Gr. 4-6
SSB1-36	Fantastic Plants Gr. 4-6
SSPC-04	Farm Animals B/W Pictures
SSB1-15	Farm Animals Gr. 1-2
SST1-03A	Farm Gr. JK/SK
SST1-03B	Farm Gr. 1
SST1-03C	Farm Gr. 2-3
SSJ1-05	Farming Community Gr. 3-4
SSB1-44	Farmyard Friends Gr. P-K
SSJ1-45	Fathers of Confederation Gr. 4-8
SSB1-19	Feathered Friends Gr. 4-6
SST1-05A	February Gr. JK/SK
SST1-05B	February Gr. 1
SST1-05C	February Gr. 2-3
SSN1-03	Festival of Fairytales Gr. 3-5
SSC1-36	Festivals Around the World Gr. 2-3
SSN1-168	First 100 Sight Words Gr. 1
SSC1-32	First Days at School Gr. 1
SSJ1-06	Fishing Community Gr. 3-4
SSN1-170	Flowers for Algernon NS Gr. 7-8
SSN1-128	Fly Away Home NS Gr. 4-6
SSD1-05	Food: Fact, Fun & Fiction Gr. 1-3
SSD1-06	Food: Nutrition & Invention Gr. 4-6
SSB1-118	Force and Motion Gr. 1-3
SSB1-119	Force and Motion Gr. 4-6
SSB1-25	Foxes Gr. 3-5
SSN1-172	Freckle Juice NS Gr. 1-3
SSB1-43	Friendly Frogs Gr. 1
SSB1-89	Fruits & Seeds Gr. 4-6
SSN1-137	Fudge-a-Mania NS Gr. 4-6
SSB1-14	Fun on the Farm Gr. 3-4
SSR1-49	Fun with Phonics Gr. 1-3
SSPC-06	Garden Flowers B/W Pictures
SSK1-03	Geometric Shapes Gr. 2-5
SSC1-18	Get the Rabbit Habit Gr. 1-2
SSN1-209	Giver, The NS Gr. 7-8
SSN1-190	Go Jump in the Pool NS Gr. 4-6
SSG1-03	Goal Setting Gr. 6-8
SSG1-08	Gr. 3 Test – Parent Guide
SSG1-99	Gr. 3 Test – Teacher Guide
SSG1-09	Gr. 6 Language Test – Parent Guide
SSG1-97	Gr. 6 Language Test – Teacher Guide
SSG1-10	Gr. 6 Math Test – Parent Guide
SSG1-96	Gr. 6 Math Test – Teacher Guide
SSG1-98	Gr. 6 Math/Lang. Test – Teacher Guide
SSK1-14	Graph for all Seasons Gr. 1-3
SSN1-117	Great Brain NS Gr. 4-6
SSN1-90	Great Expectations NS Gr. 7-8
SSN1-169	Great Gilly Hopkins NS Gr. 4-6
SSN1-197	Great Science Fair Disaster NS 4-6
SSN1-138	Greek Mythology Gr. 7-8
SSN1-113	Green Gables Detectives NS 4-6
SSC1-26	Groundhog Celebration Gr. 2
SSC1-25	Groundhog Day Gr. 1
SSB1-113	Growth & Change in Animals Gr. 2-3
SSB1-114	Growth & Change in Plants Gr. 2-3
SSB1-48	Guinea Pigs & Friends Gr. 3-5
SSB1-104	Habitats Gr. 4-6
SSPC-18	Halloween B/W Pictures
SST1-04A	Halloween Gr. JK/SK
SST1-04B	Halloween Gr. 1
SST1-04C	Halloween Gr. 2-3
SSC1-10	Halloween Gr. 4-6
SSC1-08	Halloween Happiness Gr. 1
SSC1-29	Halloween Spirits Gr. P-K
SSC1-42	Happy Valentines Day Gr. 3
SSN1-205	Harper Moon NS Gr. 7-8
SSN1-123	Harriet the Spy NS Gr. 4-6
SSC1-11	Harvest Time Wonders Gr. 1
SSN1-136	Hatchet NS Gr. 7-8
SSC1-09	Haunting Halloween Gr. 2-3
SSN1-91	Hawk & Stretch NS Gr. 4-6
SSC1-30	Hearts & Flowers Gr. P-K
SSN1-22	Heidi NS Gr. 4-6
SSN1-120	Help I'm Trapped in My NS 4-6
SSN1-24	Henry & the Clubhouse NS 4-6
SSN1-184	Hobbit NS Gr. 7-8
SSN1-122	Hoboken Chicken Emerg. NS 4-6
SSN1-250	Holes NS Gr. 4-6
SSN1-116	How Can a Frozen Detective NS 4-6
SSN1-89	How Can I be a Detective if I NS 4-6
SSN1-96	How Come the Best Clues... NS 4-6
SSN1-133	How To Eat Fried Worms NS 4-6
SSR1-48	How To Give a Presentation Gr. 4-6
SSN1-125	How To Teach Writing Through 7-9
SSR1-10	How To Write a Composition 6-10
SSR1-09	How To Write a Paragraph 5-10
SSR1-08	How To Write an Essay Gr. 7-12
SSR1-03	How To Write Poetry & Stories 4-6
SSD1-07	Human Body Gr. 2-4
SSD1-02	Human Body Gr. 4-6
SSN1-25	I Want to Go Home NS Gr. 4-6
SSH1-06	I'm Important Gr. 2-3
SSH1-07	I'm Unique Gr. 4-6

Publication Listing

Code #	Title and Grade
SSF1-05	In Days of Yore Gr. 4-6
SSF1-06	In Pioneer Days Gr. 2-4
SSM1-10	In the Wintertime Gr. 2
SSB1-41	Incredible Dinosaurs Gr. P-1
SSN1-177	Incredible Journey NS Gr. 4-6
SSN1-100	Indian in the Cupboard NS Gr. 4-6
SSPC-05	Insects B/W Pictures
SSPC-10	Inuit B/W Pictures
SSJ1-10	Inuit Community Gr. 3-4
SSN1-85	Ira Sleeps Over NS Gr. 1-3
SSN1-93	Iron Man NS Gr. 4-6
SSN1-193	Island of the Blue Dolphins NS 4-6
SSB1-11	It's a Dogs World Gr. 2-3
SSM1-05	It's a Marshmallow World Gr. 3
SSK1-05	It's About Time Gr. 2-4
SSC1-41	It's Christmas Time Gr. 3
SSH1-04	It's Circus Time Gr. 1
SSC1-43	It's Groundhog Day Gr. 3
SSB1-75	It's Maple Syrup Time Gr. 2-4
SSC1-40	It's Trick or Treat Time Gr. 2
SSN1-65	James & The Giant Peach NS 4-6
SSN1-106	Jane Eyre NS Gr. 7-8
SSPC-25	Japan B/W Pictures
SSA1-06	Japan Gr. 5-8
SSC1-05	Joy of Christmas Gr. 2
SSN1-161	Julie of the Wolves NS Gr. 7-8
SSB1-81	Jungles Gr. 2-3
SSE1-02	Junior Music for Fall Gr. 4-6
SSE1-05	Junior Music for Spring Gr. 4-6
SSE1-06	Junior Music for Winter Gr. 4-6
SSN1-151	Kate NS Gr. 4-6
SSN1-95	Kidnapped in the Yukon NS Gr. 4-6
SSN1-140	Kids at Bailey School Gr. 2-4
SSN1-176	King of the Wind NS Gr. 4-6
SSF1-29	Klondike Gold Rush Gr. 4-6
SSF1-33	Labour Movement in Canada Gr. 7-8
SSN1-152	Lamplighter NS Gr. 4-6
SSB1-98	Learning About Dinosaurs Gr. 3
SSN1-38	Learning About Giants Gr. 4-6
SSK1-22	Learning About Measurement Gr. 1-3
SSB1-46	Learning About Mice Gr. 3-5
SSK1-09	Learning About Money CDN Gr. 1-3
SSK1-19	Learning About Money USA Gr. 1-3
SSK1-23	Learning About Numbers Gr. 1-3
SSB1-69	Learning About Rocks and Soils Gr. 2-3
SSK1-08	Learning About Shapes Gr. 1-3
SSB1-100	Learning About Simple Machines 1-3
SSK1-04	Learning About the Calendar Gr. 2-3
SSK1-10	Learning About Time Gr. 1-3
SSH1-17	Learning About Transportation Gr. 1
SSB1-02	Leaves Gr. 2-3
SSN1-50	Legends Gr. 4-6
SSC1-27	Lest We Forget Gr. 4-6
SSJ1-13	Let's Look at Canada Gr. 4-6
SSJ1-16	Let's Visit Alberta Gr. 2-4
SSJ1-15	Let's Visit British Columbia Gr. 2-4
SSJ1-03	Let's Visit Canada Gr. 3
SSJ1-18	Let's Visit Manitoba Gr. 2-4
SSJ1-21	Let's Visit New Brunswick Gr. 2-4
SSJ1-27	Let's Visit Newfoundland & Labrador Gr. 2-4
SSJ1-30	Let's Visit North West Terr. Gr. 2-4
SSJ1-20	Let's Visit Nova Scotia Gr. 2-4
SSJ1-34	Let's Visit Nunavut Gr. 2-4
SSJ1-17	Let's Visit Ontario Gr. 2-4
SSQ1-08	Let's Visit Ottawa Big Book Pkg 1-3
SSJ1-19	Let's Visit PEI Gr. 2-4
SSJ1-31	Let's Visit Québec Gr. 2-4
SSJ1-14	Let's Visit Saskatchewan Gr. 2-4
SSJ1-28	Let's Visit Yukon Gr. 2-4
SSN1-130	Life & Adv. of Santa Claus NS 7-8
SSB1-10	Life in a Pond Gr. 3-4
SSF1-30	Life in the Middle Ages Gr. 7-8
SSB1-103	Light & Sound Gr. 4-6
SSN1-219	Light in the Forest NS Gr. 7-8
SSN1-121	Light on Hogback Hill NS Gr. 4-6
SSN1-46	Lion, Witch & the Wardrobe NS 4-6
SSR1-51	Literature Response Forms Gr. 1-3
SSR1-52	Literature Response Forms Gr. 4-6
SSN1-28	Little House Big Woods NS 4-6
SSN1-233	Little House on the Prairie NS 4-6
SSN1-111	Little Women NS Gr. 7-8
SSN1-115	Live from the Fifth Grade NS 4-6
SSN1-141	Look Through My Window NS 4-6
SSN1-112	Look! Visual Discrimination Gr. P-1
SSN1-61	Lost & Found NS Gr. 4-6
SSN1-109	Lost in the Barrens NS Gr. 7-8
SSJ1-08	Lumbering Community Gr. 3-4
SSN1-167	Magic School Bus Gr. 1-3
SSN1-247	Magic Treehouse Gr. 1-3
SSB1-78	Magnets Gr. 3-5
SSD1-03	Making Sense of Our Senses K-1
SSN1-146	Mama's Going to Buy You a Mocking Bird NS 4-6
SSB1-94	Mammals Gr. 1
SSB1-95	Mammals Gr. 2
SSB1-96	Mammals Gr. 3
SSB1-97	Mammals Gr. 5-6
SSN1-160	Maniac Magee NS Gr. 4-6
SSA1-19	Mapping Activities & Outlines! 4-8
SSA1-17	Mapping Skills Gr. 1-3
SSA1-07	Mapping Skills Gr. 4-6
SST1-10A	March Gr. JK/SK
SST1-10B	March Gr. 1
SST1-10C	March Gr. 2-3
SSB1-57	Marvellous Marsupials Gr. 4-6
SSK1-01	Math Signs & Symbols Gr. 1-3
SSB1-116	Matter & Materials Gr. 1-3
SSB1-117	Matter & Materials Gr. 4-6
SSH1-03	Me, I'm Special! Gr. P-1
SSK1-16	Measurement Gr. 4-8
SSC1-02	Medieval Christmas Gr. 4-6
SSPC-09	Medieval Life B/W Pictures
SSC1-07	Merry Christmas Gr. P-K
SSK1-15	Metric Measurement Gr. 4-8
SSN1-13	Mice in Literature Gr. 3-5
SSB1-70	Microscopy Gr. 4-6
SSN1-180	Midnight Fox NS Gr. 4-6
SSN1-243	Midwife's Apprentice NS Gr. 4-6
SSJ1-07	Mining Community Gr. 3-4
SSK1-17	Money Talks – Cdn Gr. 3-6
SSK1-18	Money Talks – USA Gr. 3-6
SSB1-56	Monkeys & Apes Gr. 4-6
SSN1-43	Monkeys in Literature Gr. 2-4
SSN1-54	Monster Mania Gr. 4-6
SSN1-97	Mouse & the Motorcycle NS 4-6
SSN1-94	Mr. Poppers Penguins NS Gr. 4-6
SSN1-201	Mrs. Frisby & Rats NS Gr. 4-6
SSR1-13	Milti-Level Spelling Program Gr. 3-6
SSR1-26	Multi-Level Spelling USA Gr. 3-6
SSK1-31	Addition & Subtraction Drills 1-3
SSK1-32	Multiplication & Division Drills 4-6
SSK1-30	Multiplication Drills Gr. 4-6
SSA1-14	My Country! The USA! Gr. 2-4
SSN1-186	My Side of the Mountain NS 7-8
SSN1-58	Mysteries, Monsters & Magic Gr. 6-8
SSN1-37	Mystery at Blackrock Island NS 7-8
SSN1-80	Mystery House NS 4-6
SSN1-157	Nate the Great & Sticky Case NS 1-3
SSF1-23	Native People of North America 4-6
SSF1-25	New France Part 1 Gr. 7-8
SSF1-27	New France Part 2 Gr. 7-8
SSA1-10	New Zealand Gr. 4-8
SSN1-51	Newspapers Gr. 5-8
SSN1-47	No Word for Goodbye NS Gr. 7-8
SSPC-03	North American Animals B/W Pictures
SSF1-22	North American Natives Gr. 2-4
SSN1-75	Novel Ideas Gr. 4-6
SST1-06A	November JK/SK
SST1-06B	November Gr. 1
SST1-06C	November Gr. 2-3
SSN1-244	Number the Stars NS Gr. 4-6
SSY1-03	Numeration Gr. 1-3
SSPC-14	Nursery Rhymes B/W Pictures
SSN1-12	Nursery Rhymes Gr. P-1
SSN1-59	On the Banks of Plum Creek NS 4-6
SSN1-220	One in Middle Green Kangaroo NS 1-3
SSN1-145	One to Grow On NS Gr. 4-6
SSB1-27	Opossums Gr. 3-5
SSJ1-23	Ottawa Gr. 7-9
SSJ1-39	Our Canadian Governments Gr. 5-8
SSF1-14	Our Global Heritage Gr. 4-6
SSH1-12	Our Neighbourhoods Gr. 4-6
SSB1-72	Our Trash Gr. 2-3
SSB1-51	Our Universe Gr. 5-8
SSB1-86	Outer Space Gr. 1-2
SSA1-18	Outline Maps of the World Gr. 1-8
SSB1-67	Owls Gr. 4-6
SSN1-31	Owls in the Family NS Gr. 4-6
SSL1-02	Oxbridge Owl & The Library Gr. 4-6
SSB1-71	Pandas, Polar & Penguins Gr. 4-6
SSN1-52	Paperbag Princess NS Gr. 1-3
SSR1-11	Passion of Jesus: A Play Gr. 7-8
SSA1-12	Passport to Adventure Gr. 4-5
SSR1-06	Passport to Adventure Gr. 7-8
SSR1-04	Personal Spelling Dictionary Gr. 2-5
SSPC-29	Pets B/W Pictures
SSE1-03	Phantom of the Opera Gr. 7-9
SSN1-171	Phoebe Gilman Author Study Gr. 2-3
SSY1-06	Phonics Gr. 1-3
SSN1-237	Pierre Berton Author Study Gr. 7-8
SSN1-179	Pigman NS Gr. 7-8
SSN1-48	Pigs in Literature Gr. 2-4
SSN1-99	Pinballs NS Gr. 4-6
SSN1-60	Pippi Longstocking NS Gr. 4-6
SSF1-12	Pirates Gr. 4-6
SSK1-13	Place Value Gr. 4-6
SSB1-77	Planets Gr. 3-6
SSB1-66	Popcorn Fun Gr. 2-3
SSB1-20	Porcupines Gr. 3-5
SSF1-24	Prehistoric Times Gr. 4-6
SSE1-01	Primary Music for Fall Gr. 1-3
SSE1-04	Primary Music for Spring Gr. 1-3
SSE1-07	Primary Music for Winter Gr. 1-3
SSJ1-47	Prime Ministers of Canada Gr. 4-8
SSK1-20	Probability & Inheritance Gr. 7-10
SSN1-49	Question of Loyalty NS Gr. 7-8
SSN1-26	Rabbits in Literature Gr. 2-4
SSB1-17	Raccoons Gr. 3-5
SSN1-207	Radio Fifth Grade NS Gr. 4-6
SSB1-52	Rainbow of Colours Gr. 4-6
SSN1-144	Ramona Quimby Age 8 NS 4-6
SSJ1-09	Ranching Community Gr. 3-4
SSY1-08	Reading for Meaning Gr. 1-3
SSN1-165	Reading Response Forms Gr. 1-3
SSN1-239	Reading Response Forms Gr. 4-6
SSN1-234	Reading with Arthur Gr. 1-3
SSN1-249	Reading with Canadian Authors 1-3
SSN1-200	Reading with Curious George 2-4
SSN1-230	Reading with Eric Carle Gr. 1-3
SSN1-251	Reading with Kenneth Oppel 4-6
SSN1-127	Reading with Mercer Mayer 1-2
SSN1-07	Reading with Motley Crew Gr. 2-3
SSN1-142	Reading with Robert Munsch 1-3
SSN1-06	Reading with the Super Sleuths 4-6
SSN1-08	Reading with the Ziggles Gr. 1
SST1-11A	Red Gr. JK/SK
SSN1-147	Refuge NS Gr. 7-8
SSC1-44	Remembrance Day Gr. 1-3
SSPC-23	Reptiles B/W Pictures
SSB1-42	Reptiles Gr. 4-6
SSN1-110	Return of the Indian NS Gr. 4-6
SSN1-225	River NS Gr. 7-8
SSE1-08	Robert Schuman, Composer Gr. 6-9
SSN1-83	Robot Alert NS Gr. 4-6
SSB1-65	Rocks & Minerals Gr. 4-6
SSN1-149	Romeo & Juliet NS Gr. 7-8
SSB1-88	Romping Reindeer Gr. K-3
SSN1-21	Rumplestiltskin NS Gr. 1-3
SSN1-153	Runaway Ralph NS Gr. 4-6
SSN1-103	Sadako and 1 000 Paper Cranes NS 4-6
SSD1-04	Safety Gr. 2-4
SSN1-42	Sarah Plain & Tall NS Gr. 4-6
SSC1-34	School in September Gr. 4-6
SSPC-01	Sea Creatures B/W Pictures
SSB1-79	Sea Creatures Gr. 1-3
SSN1-64	Secret Garden NS Gr. 4-6
SSB1-90	Seeds & Weeds Gr. 2-3
SSY1-02	Sentence Writing Gr. 1-3
SST1-07A	September JK/SK
SST1-07B	September Gr. 1
SST1-07C	September Gr. 2-3
SSN1-30	Serendipity Series Gr. 3-5
SSC1-22	Shamrocks on Parade Gr. 1
SSC1-24	Shamrocks, Harps & Shillelaghs 3-4
SSR1-66	Shakespeare Shorts – Performing Arts Gr. 2-4
SSR1-67	Shakespeare Shorts – Performing Arts Gr. 4-6
SSR1-68	Shakespeare Shorts – Language Arts Gr. 2-4
SSR1-69	Shakespeare Shorts – Language Arts Gr. 4-6
SSB1-74	Sharks Gr. 4-6
SSN1-158	Shiloh NS Gr. 4-6
SSN1-84	Sideways Stories Wayside NS 4-6
SSN1-181	Sight Words Activities Gr. 1
SSB1-99	Simple Machines Gr. 4-6
SSN1-19	Sixth Grade Secrets 4-6
SSG1-04	Skill Building with Slates Gr. K-8
SSN1-118	Skinny Bones NS Gr. 4-6
SSB1-24	Skunks Gr. 3-5
SSN1-191	Sky is Falling NS Gr. 4-6
SSB1-83	Slugs & Snails Gr. 1-3
SSB1-55	Snakes Gr. 4-6
SST1-12A	Snow Gr. JK/SK
SST1-12B	Snow Gr. 1
SST1-12C	Snow Gr. 2-3
SSB1-76	Solar System Gr. 4-6
SSPC-44	South America B/W Pictures
SSA1-11	South America Gr. 4-6
SSB1-05	Space Gr. 2-3
SSR1-34	Spelling Blacklines Gr. 1
SSR1-35	Spelling Blacklines Gr. 2
SSR1-14	Spelling Gr. 1
SSR1-15	Spelling Gr. 2
SSR1-16	Spelling Gr. 3
SSR1-17	Spelling Gr. 4
SSR1-18	Spelling Gr. 5
SSR1-19	Spelling Gr. 6
SSR1-27	Spelling Worksavers #1 Gr. 3-5
SSM1-02	Spring Celebration Gr. 2-3
SST1-01A	Spring Gr. JK/SK
SST1-01B	Spring Gr. 1
SST1-01C	Spring Gr. 2-3
SSM1-01	Spring in the Garden Gr. 1-2
SSB1-26	Squirrels Gr. 3-5
SSB1-112	Stable Structures and Mechanisms Gr. 3
SSG1-05	Steps in the Research Process 5-8
SSG1-02	Stock Market Gr. 7-8
SSN1-139	Stone Fox NS Gr. 4-6
SSN1-214	Stone Orchard NS Gr. 7-8
SSN1-01	Story Book Land of Witches Gr. 2-3
SSR1-64	Story Starters Gr. 1-3
SSR1-65	Story Starters Gr. 4-6
SSR1-73	Story Starters Gr. 1-6
SSY1-09	Story Writing Gr. 1-3
SSB1-111	Structures, Mechanisms and Motion Gr. 2
SSN1-211	Stuart Little NS Gr. 4-6
SSK1-29	Subtraction Drills Gr. 1-3
SSY1-05	Subtraction Gr. 1-3
SSY1-11	Successful Language Pract. Gr. 1-3
SSY1-12	Successful Math Practice Gr. 1-3
SSW1-09	Summer Learning Gr. K-1
SSW1-10	Summer Learning Gr. 1-2
SSW1-11	Summer Learning Gr. 2-3
SSW1-12	Summer Learning Gr. 3-4
SSW1-13	Summer Learning Gr. 4-5
SSW1-14	Summer Learning Gr. 5-6
SSN1-159	Summer of the Swans NS Gr. 4-6
SSZ1-02	Summer Olympics Gr. 4-6
SSM1-07	Super Summer Gr. 1-2
SSN1-18	Superfudge NS Gr. 4-6
SSA1-08	Switzerland Gr. 4-6
SSN1-20	T.V. Kid NS. Gr. 4-6
SSA1-15	Take a Trip to Australia Gr. 2-3
SSB1-102	Taking Off With Flight Gr. 1-3
SSN1-55	Tales of the Fourth Grade NS 4-6
SSN1-188	Taste of Blackberries NS Gr. 4-6
SSK1-07	Teaching Math Through Sports 6-9
SST1-09A	Thanksgiving JK/SK
SST1-09C	Thanksgiving Gr. 2-3
SSN1-77	There's a Boy in the Girls... NS 4-6
SSN1-143	This Can't Be Happening NS 4-6
SSN1-05	Three Billy Goats Gruff NS Gr. 1-3
SSN1-72	Ticket to Curlew NS Gr. 4-6
SSN1-82	Timothy of the Cay NS Gr. 7-8
SSF1-32	Titanic Gr. 4-6
SSN1-222	To Kill a Mockingbird NS Gr. 7-8
SSN1-195	Toilet Paper Tigers NS Gr. 4-6
SSJ1-35	Toronto Gr. 4-8
SSH1-02	Toy Shelf Gr. P-K
SSPC-24	Toys B/W Pictures
SSN1-163	Traditional Poetry Gr. 7-10
SSH1-13	Transportation Gr. 4-6
SSW1-01	Transportation Snip Art
SSB1-03	Trees Gr. 2-3
SSA1-01	Tropical Rainforest Gr. 4-6
SSN1-56	Trumpet of the Swan NS Gr. 4-6
SSN1-81	Tuck Everlasting NS Gr. 4-6
SSN1-126	Turtles in Literature Gr. 1-3
SSN1-45	Underground to Canada NS 4-6
SSN1-27	Unicorns in Literature Gr. 3-5
SSJ1-44	Upper & Lower Canada Gr. 7-8
SSN1-192	Using Novels Canadian North Gr. 7-8
SSC1-14	Valentines Day Gr. 5-8
SSPC-45	Vegetables B/W Pictures
SSY1-01	Very Hungry Caterpillar NS 30/Pkg 1-3
SSF1-13	Victorian Era Gr. 7-8
SSC1-35	Victorian Christmas Gr. 5-8
SSF1-17	Viking Age Gr. 4-6
SSN1-206	War with Grandpa SN Gr. 4-6
SSB1-91	Water Gr. 2-4
SSN1-166	Watership Down NS Gr. 7-8
SSH1-16	Ways We Travel Gr. P-K
SSN1-101	Wayside School Gets a Little Stranger NS 4-6

Code #	Title and Grade
SSN1-76	Wayside School is Falling Down NS 4-6
SSB1-60	Weather Gr. 4-6
SSN1-17	Wee Folk in Literature Gr. 3-5
SSPC-08	Weeds B/W Pictures
SSQ1-04	Welcome Back – Big Book Pkg 1-3
SSB1-73	Whale Preservation Gr. 5-8
SSH1-08	What is a Community? Gr. 2-4
SSH1-01	What is a Family? Gr. 2-3
SSH1-09	What is a School? Gr. 1-2
SSJ1-32	What is Canada? Gr. P-K
SSN1-79	What is RAD? Read and Discover 2-4
SSB1-62	What is the Weather Today? Gr. 2-4
SSN1-194	What's a Daring Detective NS 4-6
SSH1-10	What's My Number Gr. P-K
SSR1-02	What's the Scoop on Words Gr. 4-6
SSN1-73	Where the Red Fern Grows NS 7-8
SSN1-87	Where the Wild Things Are NS 1-3
SSN1-187	Whipping Boy NS Gr. 4-6
SSN1-226	Who is Frances Rain? NS Gr. 4-6
SSN1-74	Who's Got Gertie & How...? NS 4-6
SSN1-131	Why did the Underwear ... NS 4-6
SSC1-28	Why Wear a Poppy? Gr. 2-3
SSJ1-11	Wild Animals of Canada Gr. 2-3
SSPC-07	Wild Flowers B/W Pictures
SSB1-18	Winter Birds Gr. 2-3
SSZ1-03	Winter Olympics Gr. 4-6
SSM1-04	Winter Wonderland Gr. 1
SSC1-01	Witches Gr. 3-4
SSN1-213	Wolf Island NS Gr. 1-3
SSE1-09	Wolfgang Amadeus Mozart 6-9
SSB1-23	Wolves Gr. 3-5
SSC1-20	Wonders of Easter Gr. 2
SSB1-35	World of Horses Gr. 4-6
SSB1-13	World of Pets Gr. 2-3
SSF1-26	World War II Gr. 7-8
SSN1-221	Wrinkle in Time NS Gr. 7-8
SSPC-02	Zoo Animals B/W Pictures
SSB1-08	Zoo Animals Gr. 1-2
SSB1-09	Zoo Celebration Gr. 3-4

Code #	Title and Grade

Code #	Title and Grade

Code #	Title and Grade